A
PRISONER OF FRANCE

THE

MEMOIRS, DIARY, AND CORRESPONDENCE
OF CHARLES BOOTHBY, CAPTAIN
ROYAL ENGINEERS, DURING
HIS LAST CAMPAIGN

LONDON
ADAM AND CHARLES BLACK
1898

Charles Brokkby
Capitaine Anglais
Prisonnier de guerre

LIST OF ILLUSTRATIONS

PEN-AND-INK SKETCHES

From the Author's Journals

327127

INTRODUCTION

CHARLES BOOTHBY, third son of Sir William
Boothby, Bart., and Dame Rafela, his wife, was
born at Dublin in 1786. After a few years at
the well-known school of Uppingham, he was
sent to the Royal Military Academy, Woolwich.
Having passed the examination there, he joined
the Royal Engineers. His first year of service
was spent uneventfully on a home station. Early
in 1805 his career began in earnest. He was
then ordered for foreign service under Sir James
Craig, with whom he took part in the campaign
at Naples. Next year he served under Sir John
Stuart in Calabria, sharing in the battle of Maida
and in other military operations, for which all the
officers received the thanks of Parliament—those
of the Royal Engineers the especial thanks.
Afterwards, for a short time, Boothby was employed in Sicily. Twice he was sent on services
of reconnaissance on the enemy's coast by Major
Lefebure, who made written acknowledgment of

the young soldier's "zealous, unremitting, and useful professional support." When Sir John Moore commanded in Sicily, Boothby, by that time a Captain, was entrusted with the task of preparing the fortress of Augusta for immediate defence. Towards the end of 1807 he left Sicily, under Captain Burgoyne, with an Expedition to Portugal conducted by Sir John Moore. The Expedition was too late to accomplish the purpose with which it started, and was back in England in January 1808.

Boothby's inactivity lasted only for a brief space. Early in the spring of the same year he sailed for Sweden, under Captain Squire, with the army of Sir John Moore, and surveyed an island in the Great Belt, which, if necessary, was to be fortified. Home again in July, he followed Sir John Moore to Portugal, put himself under the orders of Lieutenant-Colonel Fletcher at Cintra, and, as he himself wrote, "assisted in the laborious duties of forming topographical documents of the kingdom of Portugal." When Moore advanced into Spain, in the same year, Boothby was attached to the reserve, which was commanded by General Paget, and made journeys in search of information about the roads and the regions over which the army was to pass. He was also employed, in advance, in estimating the enemy's strength and watching his movements. After the retreat he was despatched by the Commander-in-Chief on confidential service ; after which he embarked at Vigo, and rejoined the army at Corunna. At the battle there, on the 16th of January 1809, he assisted in the construction of the works thrown up to cover the embarkation of the troops which was to ensue. In England, at the end of the month, again, with his comrades-in-arms, Boothby received the thanks of Parliament.

Early in March he accompanied Lieutenant-Colonel Fletcher to Portugal, in which Sir Arthur Wellesley had assumed the command. In the combined operations upon Oporto he served with a British Brigade under Marshal Beresford, who commanded the native troops. Immediately afterwards he joined the British army at Abrantes, and was attached to General Sherbrooke, second in command.

From that time onwards, in the narrative which follows, Captain Boothby's adventures in war time are told in his own words. In these present days, when it seems not improbable that the century, according to the habit of centuries, will die in flames, Captain Boothby's story of the adversities of war, and of the courtesies of the enemy by which they were mitigated, will be read with lively interest. Boothby himself, unfortunately, when at length he was free to quit the Continent, was no longer able to serve his country on any battlefield; but his disposition was too much towards activity to permit of his being a recluse. Soon after his return home, still a young man, he entered at St. Mary's Hall, Oxford; took a degree; and was ordained deacon by the Bishop of Salisbury. By and by Lord Liverpool presented him to the Crown living of Sutterton, in Lincolnshire, which he held for nearly thirty years, until his death, in 1846. During that incumbency, through the patronage of Archbishop Venables Vernon Harcourt, he became a Residentiary Canon of Southwell Minster, and that enabled him to hold also the living of Barnoldby-le-Beck. Married to Marianne Catherine Beridge, third daughter of the Rev. Basil B. Beridge, rector of Algarkirk, he left seven children. He was for many years Chairman of Quarter Sessions in the Holland Division of Lincolnshire.

In all his various capacities Boothby was highly esteemed. Perhaps we cannot more fitly close this outline of his career than by quoting the written words of one who had the privilege of being personally acquainted with him. "I had the pleasure," Lady Bloomfield says, "of knowing the Rev. Charles Boothby very well when I was a girl. He was an intimate friend of my mother, Lady Ravensworth. We always looked forward with pleasure to his visits at Percy's Cross.

He had charming manners, and was a remarkably handsome man, with a most benevolent countenance and a sweet smile which was particularly winning to children. He had a cork leg and was rather lame, which used to excite my sympathy ; but his gentle manners, unvarying kindness, and warm affection, have left an impression on my mind which the lapse of many years since his lamented death has not obliterated. It is with pleasure that I record the memory of one whom I loved and respected."

A PRISONER OF FRANCE

CHAPTER I

ON the 27th July 1809 the division of General Sherbrooke retired across the river Alverche : General Cuesta had withdrawn the Spaniards from the bridge on our right flank. The confidence of the allies seemed now converted into apprehension — I speak in a military sense, not referring to the personal fears of individuals, which in a British army have no place.

The fact of General Wellesley's having determined to entrench himself at Talavera, for which there was no premeditation, indicated that the confidence by which he had been buoyed up was changed into the resolution sometimes imparted by despair, or at least that he considered himself inferior to the enemy.

Soon General Sherbrooke entered the town ; and, he having no immediate occasion for my services, I was at liberty to provide quarters for myself and stabling for my horses. One very old woman, Doña Pollonia di Monton, was the only human being left in the house to which the magistracy of the town had directed me. Its other inhabitants, alarmed by the return of the British and their countrymen in arms, had fled to the mountains, leaving this venerable dame as the best protection for their dwelling, she being too old and decrepit to provoke desire or awaken ferocity.

She received me with the civility of fear, spoke of the French officers with respect and praise, and, when I told her I was an Englishman, expressed her disbelief by a wistful smile and an incredulous movement of her head. She was much relieved when convinced of my sincerity, but, still preparing herself for troubles, supplied my wants with an air of distrustful melancholy.

Having desired Pedro, my Italian servant, to prepare dinner, I went out to be in the way of information. The town presented a scene of dislocation and alarm that would be difficult to describe. Reports rose up like exhalations, passing from one to another in rapid succession, extending terror and confusion. At one moment : "The French had possession of the suburbs!" The inhabitants ran through the streets with as much anguish in their faces as if they already felt the bayonets in their bodies. At another : "The

British general was in full march to Oropesa!"
"O dios! los Ingleses nos abandonan!" "Jesus!
Maria! Jose! los Ingleses nos abandonan!"

As the day waned, the occasional sound of
cannon announced our contact with the enemy.
Tired of being the sport of idle rumour, I mounted
my little mule, and, ordering my batman not to
stir with my horses until he heard from me, I rode
towards the position occupied by the army. I had
no expectation of an action that evening; for it is a
rule of war that, except in cases of surprise, it is
ill-judged to direct a night attack. I concluded
that the skirmishing would cease with the light, and
that the French would engage us at daybreak.
For that hour, therefore, I wished my chargers to
be fresh, expecting to return after dark in time to
take the refreshment that I needed. With these
ideas I rode to the field, where everything wore
the most hostile appearance. The enemy in our
front, having driven in the outposts, had begun a
heavy and well-directed cannonade upon our whole
line. I immediately sought for General Sherbrooke, who, as but few of his staff were then near
him, was glad of my timely arrival, and gave me
full employment in making known or in executing his intentions. The cannon of the enemy
were spiritedly and effectually answered by ours,
although we were contending with heavier metal.
This encountering thunder, however, ceased with

the light, and an awful pause accompanied the fall of evening.

We peered anxiously through the thick dusk, and could see the French columns, deliberate and silent, approaching the brow of the opposite hill. Noticing the light infantry which we had thrown out in front collected in a body and apparently waiting the enemy's approach, I said to General Sherbrooke that I feared the intention was misunderstood. If, on being pushed, they fell back in a body, they would either be taken for the enemy and destroyed, or break our line and throw it into confusion. The General acquiesced in my observation, and desired me to find out the officer commanding and explain his wishes. Away I went, but found that what I had taken for a body of soldiers was a thicket, and that, in fact, the light infantry were disposed, as the very intelligent and brave officer commanding was sure to dispose them, to the best advantage.

I fell in with Captain Blair, who also had been sent to that officer, and just as we had recognised each other a volleying began from our left. It instantly struck us both that in the confusion of night the fire would spread down the whole line, in which case we should be blown to pieces.

Under this impression, I clapped spurs to my mule, and pushed her to her utmost speed. But the blaze from the left came down with greater speed, and before I could reach the line I found myself galloping up to an uninterrupted sheet of fire.

I had just time enough to think my escape impossible before I was struck in the leg by a musket ball, which brought me to the ground.

As the firing continued, I conceived that the enemy was at hand, and got up; but my leg doubled under me, and I had to creep through the ranks on my hands and knees.

A sergeant who was posted in the rear offered to carry me to a distance if I could get upon his back. I made the attempt; but, exhausted with pain and loss of blood, fell from his shoulders and fainted.

On coming to myself, I seemed as in bed, slowly waking from a deep sleep; but my foot was stagnated and full of pain. Instead of this sensation going off, it increased to a very violent degree; and I was beginning to be very much puzzled, when the firing on both sides, and the wondrous scene on which I opened my eyes, awoke me to a consciousness of the reality. The same sergeant was still standing over me, and I again asked him if he could not remove me. Having his halbert and knapsack, he said there was no other way but by my getting on his back. That I could not do.

Ere long the line was a little advanced; and my friend the sergeant told me that the enemy was driven back, which was on many accounts a consolation, for had the troops behind which I lay

(Germans) been overthrown, my fate must have been deplorable.

The firing had now subsided, and only a little irregular sharp-shooting was to be heard. An officer rode towards me, and a voice which I knew to be Blair's exclaimed, " O, my dear Boothby, is that you ? " I asked him if he could get me a surgeon, and he rode off. I afterwards found that poor Blair was speaking to me from the ground, where he lay wounded, near me, and that the mounted officer must have been some other person. Soon after an officer rode past, whom, to my great comfort, I distinguished to be General Sherbrooke. I called to him ; and, turning back, he expressed much sorrow at finding me in that plight, inquired into the nature of my wound, and immediately ordered up from the reserve four men and a bier to carry me to the town of Talavera. The road lay for two miles through a wood which joined the skirts of the town. It was dark ; and, being encumbered with their arms and accoutrements, the men who were to carry me were but barely sufficient for their load. Their irregular motion, grating the bones of my shattered leg, gave me excruciating pain ; and I should again have become insensible had not one of them put his canteen of wine to my mouth as he saw me growing faint—thus bestowing, with noble liberality, what at such a time was almost as precious to him as his blood.

I was oppressed with heat, and, to gain a freer respiration, took off my stock and bared my throat to the night air ; my hat was left in the field.   In our passage through the wood the men were frequently alarmed, and, notwithstanding my entreaties, set me several times on the ground, to go in quest of the bushes or stumps of trees which the night-breeze made vocal, and darkness to the eye of apprehension presented as lurking enemies. This proceeding gave me great disturbance. Whenever they put me down in the middle of that wood, I had no security for their return, especially as they had taken it into their heads that Talavera was in the hands of the French, and that my persisting in being carried thither was very unreasonable. I was also afraid that, being so long without medical assistance, I might bleed to death ; and the action of putting me down and again raising me up (unavoidable on their part) tortured me.

Those four soldiers, however, had too much honesty to abandon me ; but a misfortune almost as distressing occurred.   They lost their way.   Of the paths that went through the wood they knew not which to choose.   One proposed the left-hand path.   Another having assured him that that path led to the enemy's camp, they were proceeding on that to the right, when I desired them to stop.   Raising my shoulders above the bier, I roused my languid perceptions, and looked attentively round me. I saw then a strong haze of light over the wood, in the direction of the left-hand path, and told the men that it must come from Talavera ; but they all insisted that the light came from the camp of our enemies. Desiring them to be perfectly silent, I strained my ear to catch some guiding sound. Then I could plainly distinguish the chiming of clocks, the barking of dogs, and the buzz of populace, that came from where the light was, in a mingled drowsy hum.

The men were now convinced. Had I not been able to make the effort of putting them right, the consequences of their mistake might have proved melancholy indeed. We fell in with several Spaniards, whom, probably, the shelter of night had tempted to listen to the fears which withdrew them from their ranks. These confirmed us in our road, and reassured my bearers by information that the town remained tranquil and secure.

At the skirts of the town they rested near some reserve guns commanded by an officer of artillery whom I knew. It gave me pleasure to see a friend ; but to him, I do believe, the meeting was much less agreeable. I asked for the artillery surgeon, but was told he was in the field. The officer pointed out the way to the general hospital ; and soon after we fell in with a straggling Spaniard who conducted us thither. We arrived at nine o'clock—about three hours after I had received my wound. I cannot express the anxiety that was taken off my mind to find myself at last in the hands of the surgeon. I now felt that my part was performed, and resigned myself. Mr. Higgins, Mr. Bell, and other surgeons (then all unknown to me) were busily employed in attending such as had suffered in the destructive cannonade which began the action. Upon my saying that I had a lodging in the town, they agreed that I had better be carried thither immediately, and Mr. Bell readily offered to accompany me. The further exertion of directing the way to my quarters through the intricate streets of the town was still required of me. . Fortunately, I remembered the name of my host, Don Manoel di Monton, and of the street where he lived, Calle de las conchas ; by which means the house was ascertained, and I was carried upstairs. .

The lively manner in which the old lady (who had in the morning taken me for a Frenchman) was affected has left an indelible impression upon my memory.

"What ?" she exclaimed, while the tears ran down her furrowed cheeks. "Can this be the same ? This he whose cheeks in the morning were glowing with health ?[1] Blessed Virgin, see how white they are now ! "

---

[1] *Color de rosa* was the expression of the old woman : the Spaniards are generally so sallow that to them the colour which we ourselves consider as the natural attendant of youth and health is an object of admiration.

She made haste to prepare a bed. Oh! what
a luxury to be laid upon it after the hours of
pain ·and anxiety, almost hopeless, I had undergone!

Mr. Bell cut off my boot, and, having examined the wound, said, "Sir, I fear there is no
chance of saving your leg, and the amputation
must be above the knee."

The idea of losing a leg in the heyday of
youth could not but be painful; but it was the
less shocking as I had prepared my mind for a
more awful separation, for I am far from putting
a limb in competition with life; nor, I conceive,
can any one do so who loves and is beloved in the
world.

> For who, to dumb forgetfulness a prey,
>   This pleasing anxious being e'er resigned,
> Left the warm precincts of the cheerful day,
>   Nor cast one longing, ling'ring look behind?

I demanded of the surgeon if danger were to
be apprehended from delay.

He answered that the sooner the operation was
performed the better, but that it could not be until
morning; and, upon my expressing a wish to have
another opinion as to its necessity, he admitted that
to be very natural.

I passed a night of excruciating pain, which no
effort of my mind could enable me to bear with

patience.   My groans were faint, because my body
was exhausted.

Poor Mr. Bell, who slept in a bed near to mine,
did not, I fear, enjoy uninterrupted rest.   I called
to him before daylight to know if it was not time
to see the surgeons, and gave my unabating
torments as an excuse for disturbing him.   At
dawn he went to the hospital, promising to return
with Mr. Higgins.   Daylight was ushered in by a
roar of cannon so loud, so continuous, so tremendous, that I hardly conceived the wars of all
the earth, with united voice, could produce such a
wild and illimitable din.   Every shot seemed to
shake the house with increasing violence ; and
poor Doña Pollonia, rushing into the room with
every gesture of distraction, exclaimed, " They
are firing the town !   They are firing the town ! "

" No, no," said I.   " Don't be frightened.   Why
should they fire the town ?   Don't you perceive
that the firing is more distant and less frequent ? "

The poor woman acknowledged that it was ;
and, seeming surprised at my calmness, when she
thought that I had more right to be alarmed
than herself, she became less distraught and
watched by me with sympathising sorrow.   The
next-door neighbour, a carpenter named Augustin,
had been called in to sit with me.   He was himself ill of a fever, and suffering much.   Finding
the day advancing, my pains unabating, and no

signs of any medical assistance, I tore a leaf from my pocket-book, and with a pencil wrote a note to Mr. Higgins, saying that, as I had been informed no time was to be lost in the amputation, I was naturally anxious that my case should be as soon as possible attended to. Giving this note to Augustin, I desired him to wait at the hospital until Mr. Higgins was ready, and then to show him the way. My messenger soon returned, saying that the surgeon could not possibly leave the hospital.

I sent a second note, and a third ; and towards ten o'clock the harassed surgeon made his appearance.

"Captain Boothby," said he, "I am extremely sorry that I could not possibly come here before— still more sorry that I only come now to tell you I cannot serve you. There is but one case of instruments, which it is impossible for me to bring from the hospital while crowds of wounded, both officers and men, are pressing for assistance."

Feeling all the reasonableness of this manly explanation, I said I did but wish to take my turn.

"I hope," added he, "that towards evening the crowd will decrease, and that I shall be able to bring Mr. Gunning with me to consult upon your case and do for you whatever may be thought necessary."

"Will you examine my wound, sir," said I,

" and tell me honestly whether you apprehend any danger from the delay thus become necessary ? "

He examined my leg, and said, after a pause—

" No. I see nothing in this case from which the danger would be increased by waiting five or six hours."

There was nothing for it, therefore, but patience, which is rarely the attendant of violent pain. I taxed my mind to make an effort : I endeavoured to recall the manliness of my previous reflections— to fling myself on beyond the present afflicted hour —and to bethink me how despicable and unimportant pain seems when only the remembrance of it remains. But Pain, far from loosening his fangs at the suggestions of reason, clung fast, and persisted in teaching me that, in spite of mental pride, he is and must be dreadful to the human frame.

When I inquired for my two servants, I found that, guided by some false rumour, or struck with panic fright, they had left the town with my horses the evening before, notwithstanding my injunctions to the contrary.

Aaron, my batman, who was a soldier, finding that he had been deceived, proceeded on the 28th to the field of battle, very naturally supposing that I should be distressed about my horses ; but soon, hearing that I was wounded, he made the best of his way to my quarters.

Mr. Higgins, as he had given me to expect, came to me about three o'clock, bringing with him Mr. Gunning and Mr. Bell, and such instruments as they might have occasion for. Mr. Gunning sat down by my bedside, and made a formal exhortation: explained that to save the life it was necessary to part with the limb, and required of me an effort of the mind and a manly resolution. I interrupted him by telling him that whatever the surgeons thought necessary I should abide by; that I placed myself in their hands, being incompetent to exercise a judgment on the matter; and that they might depend upon me—as I could upon myself—as equal to any pain that was unavoidable. Then the surgeons, having examined my wound, went to another part of the room to consult; after which they withdrew—to bring the apparatus, I imagined. Hours passed without bringing their return; and Aaron, having sought Mr. Gunning, was told that he was too much occupied. This after having warned me that there was no time to be lost!

"Go, then," said I, "again into the street, and bring hither the first medical officer you happen to fall in with."

He soon returned, bringing with him Mr. Grasset, surgeon of the 48th Regiment.

I stated to Mr. Grasset the source of my impatience. Upon examining my wound, he declared that he was by no means convinced of the necessity of the amputation, and would on no account under-taken the responsibility of so serious a measure, without consultation.

"But," said I, "I suppose an attempt to save the leg will be attended with great danger ?"

"So will the amputation," answered Mr. Grasset; "but we must hope for the best, and I see nothing to make your cure impossible. The bones, to be sure, are much shattered, and the leg is much mangled and swollen; but that may all suppurate and come right, so that I cannot think of amputating without more advice. But have you been bled, sir ?" he asked.

"No," said I.

Mr. Grasset conceived bleeding absolutely necessary, and at my request he bled me in the arm.

For some moments the hope of saving my limb, which he had given me, glanced a ray of comfort into my breast; but unrelenting pain soon took from me all consciousness but of misery, all power but that of groaning.

The opinion of Mr. Grasset was the more remarkable, if sincere, because Mr. Gunning's departure (which to me seemed unaccountable) proceeded from his conviction that a gangrene had already begun, and that it would be cruel, as he expressed himself to Mr. Higgins, to disturb my dying moments by a painful and fruitless operation.

As I had taken nothing but vinegar and water since my misfortune, my strength was exhausted, and the operation of bleeding was succeeded by an interval of painful unconsciousness. From this state I was roused in the evening by Captain Craig, General Sherbrooke's aide-de-camp, who had himself been slightly wounded in the arm. He came to inquire after me and to bring me comfort, having met Mr. Grasset, who had repeated to him the opinion that he had delivered to me. I told Craig that Mr. Grasset's opinion did not give me much consolation, but that if he could find Fitz-Patrick and send him to me, I should then know my fate, as in him I placed the utmost confidence, both as a surgeon and a friend. "But who," I demanded, "has gained the day?"

The aide-de-camp then told me that, after a bloody contest, the French had been completely beaten, and had fled beyond the Alverche, with the loss of three eagles and twenty pieces of cannon.

Spent as I was, the comfort and life this account poured into my breast it is quite impossible for me to describe. For some moments I forgot my suffering in the swell of exultation, and heard of the slaughter and repulse of the confident foe with a smile of vindictive triumph. But many men that I knew had fallen to rise no more!

Many also were wounded, and suffering like myself. But if I am capable of charitable sorrow for
the suffering of others, I fear I am not insensible
to the comfort which arises from participated
calamity. That "social sorrow loses half its pain"
is a reproach to human nature from which I would
willingly withdraw myself; but, whatever I might
do with others, I could not deceive myself. I felt
it to be just.

When Craig left me I relapsed into that
troubled stupor in which consciousness of being
is only retained by the violence of bodily pain.
From this state I was roused by some one taking
hold of my hand. It was FitzPatrick.

DoÑa Pollonia,
"*Van encender la villa!*"

2

CHAPTER II

"IF I had you in London," said FitzPatrick with a sigh, as he looked at my shattered limb, "I might attempt to save it, but amid the present circumstances it would be hopeless."

"Then be it as it may. Now that I am in your hands, I am content."

"Those who told me of your wound said also that the amputation had been performed; else, ill as I could have been spared, I would have left the field and come to you."

"Do you think you are come too late?" I asked.

He said "No"; but he dissembled. At that time I was under strong symptoms of lock-jaw, which did not disappear until many hours after the amputation.

"Then, when will you operate?"

"To-morrow morning. We must have daylight."

"Could you not give me something to alleviate my sufferings, which are scarce supportable?"

He took a towel, and, soaking it in vinegar and water, laid it on my wound ; which gave me considerable relief.

He stayed with me till late, changing the lotion as often as its cooling properties were mastered by the heat of inflammation.

I passed another dismal night, and hailed the morning beam as bringing the promise of some change—sure that my pains could not be augmented.

FitzPatrick and Miller of the Artillery, Higgins and Bell, staff-surgeons, were the gentlemen who at nine o'clock prepared to perform this serious operation upon me. Having laid out the necessary instruments, they put a table in the middle of the room and placed on it a mattress. Then one of the surgeons came to me and exhorted me to summon my fortitude. I told him that he need not be afraid ; and FitzPatrick stopped him, saying that he could answer for me. They then took me to the table and laid me on the mattress. Mr. Miller wished to place a handkerchief over my eyes ; but I assured him that it was unnecessary— I would look another way. The tornequet being adjusted, I saw that the knife was in FitzPatrick's hand ; which being as I wished, I averted my head.

As I do not choose to gratify the curious (at the expense of the feeling) reader, I shall not

describe an operation the details of which are perhaps even more shocking to reflect upon than to
experience. But, as it is a common idea that the
most painful part of an amputation lies in sunder-
ing the bone, I may rectify an error by declaring
that the only part of the process in which the pain
comes up to the natural anticipation is the first
incision round the limb, by which the skin is
divided—the sensation of which is as if a prodigious weight were impelling the severing edge.
The sawing of the bone gives no uneasy sensation ;
or, if any, it is overpowered by others more
violent.

" Is it off ? " said I, as I felt it separate.

" Yes," said FitzPatrick. " Your sufferings
are over."

" Ah, no! You have yet to take up the
arteries ! "

" It will give you no pain," he said, kindly ;
and that was true—at least, after what I had
undergone, the pain seemed nothing.

I was carried back to my bed, free from pain,
but much exhausted. The surgeons complimented
me upon my firmness, and I felt gratified that I
had gone through what lay before me without
flinching, or admitting a thought of cowardly
despair. I desired that the amputated limb might
be brought to me, that I might examine the wound.
This request was opposed with some force by the

surgeons ; but I persisted, and found a certain satisfaction in observing that the limb wore an appearance to the last degree mangled and hopeless. This moderated my tender sorrow at beholding for the last time that active and invaluable servant.

Now that my body was released from pain, my mind attempted to resume a cheerful tone. Hope returned to my breast, and all the fond scenes with which fancy decorates the prospect of youth began again to gleam through the clouds of misfortune. Much was lost ; but when all was going, and the gloomy screen of oblivion seemed ready to fall between me and the world, to have saved so much—to have preserved the possibility of yet being given back to happiness and friendship—silenced my regrets, and awakened thankfulness. Reader, if thou hast a friend who is near to thy heart, and in the hour of sickness and affliction he has held up thy head, watched over, and fed, and tended thee as a father his child, thou wilt know that the balm of such a solace enters the heart with so sweet an infusion of peace, as makes it difficult to regret the calamity which has taught thee such heavenly sensations.

> Some feelings are to mortals given,
> With less of earth in them than heaven.

I shall dilate no further upon the pleasure I

derived from the constant attendance, day and night, of Edmund Mulcaster, for whom my affection had grown with our growth and strengthened with our strength.   Adorned with all the qualities that demand praise, and the modesty that shrinks from it, now is not the time to delineate his character, nor is mine the hand that can do it impartially. This officer could scarce be persuaded to leave me even for the shortest intervals.   For some time after the operation my dangerous symptoms increased.   My stomach refused sustenance, and a constant hiccough was recognised by the surgeons as a fatal prognostic.   This faithful friend never left my bedside to take himself that rest which a constant state of previous fatigue rendered so needful to him.   I urged the danger of making indispensable to me a constant attendance which it would not be in his power to give, and assured him that I was more at ease when I knew that he was refreshing himself, more especially as his was an ardent spirit, much too active for a delicate frame.

General Sherbrooke was no longer my General, but an affectionate and sympathising friend, or rather a protecting parent.   He came to me often, anticipated all my wants, and evinced the most earnest anxiety for my preservation.

Indeed, the kindness and anxiety expressed by the companions who now surrounded my bed, the exhilaration of victory, and the watchful minister-

ing of my friend, offered a charm of consolation
that I cordially wish to any sufferer whose misfortunes may resemble mine; a charm which, I
believe, encouraged my wavering powers to rally,
and cleared the channels to receive the refluent
stream of life.

There had run a report that my campaigning
chum, a *sweet-blooded lad*[1] of eighteen, had been
cut down by the enemy's cavalry, which had
caused me much uneasiness, for I was sincerely
attached to him. The falsehood of this report was
evinced to me in a most agreeable manner by his
appearance at my bedside, safe and sound. His
attendant, a faithful Highlander, really had been
cut down. His skilful arm was overcome by
numbers, and his master was preserved by the
fleetness of his horse.

He softly demanded if there was anything in
the world he could do to serve or comfort me.

General Sherbrooke, Richard Stewart, and my
kind friend and chief, Colonel Fletcher, had all
written to my friends; but, thinking that a few
words from myself would be a greater comfort to
those loved and afflicted beings, I made my young
friend sit down, and dictated a letter to my mother,
in which I directed them to hope for the best, and
to resign themselves cheerfully to what was irre-

---

[1] Dr. Moore, in speaking of his son (afterwards so well known and so
widely lamented), was in the habit of saying, " *Jack is a sweet-blooded lad.*"

trievable. I signed the letter myself; and, having made this effort to mitigate their pain, I felt less trouble on their account. The feeling reader will not impute disingenuousness to me when I describe my apprehensions and my regrets as deriving most of their poignancy from the deep affliction and alarm into which I knew my relations would be plunged by the news of my misfortune. A man need not be vain of the love of his father and mother : it is not measured by his merit, nor by the return that he makes to it : it is boundless as the beneficence of Heaven, which flows unchecked upon the unworthiness of mankind.

On the 30th, Pedro, my Italian servant, returned. He ran to me, saying, " O, my master— my dear master ! "

My most unfavourable symptom was the refusal of my stomach to retain any sort of nutriment. In the night of the 30th, however, by the perseverance of Mulcaster, I managed to retain some mulled wine, strongly spiced, and in the morning I took two eggs from the same welcome hand. This was the " turn." My unfavourable symptoms subsided, and the flowing stream of life began to replenish by degrees its almost deserted channels. So I had continued to improve until August 2, when some officers, entering my room, said that information had been received of Soult's arrival with a considerable force at Placentia, and that

General Wellesley intended to head back and engage him.

Nothing was now heard of but the crushing of Soult between Beresford and Wellesley. To some it seemed a nice thing to have got him into such a trap; but to me it carried a more melancholy reflection. I regarded the British General as out-manœuvred, and considered our blood as flowing fruitlessly. I felt that I must be left, that I must part with the most precious alleviation to my misfortunes, and become the booty of the enemy. To this reverse, bitter as it was, I immediately began to reconcile my mind. I was in a fair way of recovery. I might have more troubles to encounter; but, after all, the end might possibly be well. General Sherbrooke supplied me with whatever money I desired, and sent me some bottles of port wine and claret, a present of which the benefit was incalculable. He brought with him Colonel M'Kennon of the Guards.

"Boothby," said he, "Colonel M'Kennon is to be left in charge of Talavera. When you are fit to move, he will take you to his quarters, which are those I am quitting. You will be cooler and more comfortable there than you are here."

"If the French come while we are away, Boothby," said Goldfinch, "you must cry out, 'Capitaine Anglais,' and you will be treated well. In the very fury of the storm at Oporto, that title recommended me to their courtesy and respect."

On August 3 my friends all took leave of me with the most affectionate kindness. It was a blank, rugged moment. I had to part with my friend Mulcaster. He took both my hands. I could not speak. It was wresting from me more than may be told. But the hard hand of adversity is the best teacher of submission, and though patience is powerless to preserve us from affliction, undoubtedly it moderates the pressure.

FitzPatrick stayed till the 4th. In the morning he promised to engage for me the attendance of Mr. Higgins, who was left the senior surgeon ; expressed great regret at leaving me behind, and promised to see me again before he left the town ; but he was prevented by rumours that the French were approaching, which spread a general panic terror, and induced him to depart suddenly.

A Mountain Church in Old Castile (p. 248).

CHAPTER III[1]

THE mass of the people of England is hasty and often unjust in its judgment of military events. Reported success gives them undue exultation, and if any reverse ensue they sink as much as they rose. This indiscretion on the part of the people causes uphill work for the Generals of England. Instead of feeling any fondness for her bold sons, who to gain her approbation brave death and give up the luxuries of life—instead of feeling a parental concern for their honour and credit, and a consequent reluctance to see their faults—the people are often ready not only to blame them for disaster, but also to impute success to Fortune, and failure to their want of skill. The demon of discord also, or, as we name him, Party, extends his baneful influence over the fortunes of our heroes. Often half the nation condemns a General as rash when he advances; the other half

[1] This chapter was written the year after the battle of Talavera. The subsequent career of the Duke of Wellington has placed him on an eminence which no blame and no common praise can reach—up to which, indeed, I now look with English sentiments of exultation and gratitude.

reviles him as a coward when he retreats. It follows that it is an indispensable duty for a British General to drive from his heart all expectation of popular applause. Let his own judgment be his perpetual guide, and the good and the glory of his country his perpetual object. Should folly, ignorance, or prejudice deprive him of applause, be his sweetest consolation the certainty of having deserved it.

Such was the conduct of Moore!

News of the battle of Talavera was announced by the trumpet of victory. The people of England, elated by the sound, expected the emancipation of Spain. In the same measure as they had been raised above the mark were they cast down below it when told that the victors had been obliged to retire and leave their wounded to the mercy of a vanquished enemy. They thought they had been deceived by the earlier report, instead of by their own enthusiasm ; and few English citizens will now bear to hear of the victory of Talavera. Yet never was a victory more decided—never was the amazing preponderance of British valour more splendidly demonstrated. And this is the ground of triumph —let who will deplore the loss of Spain, when she *is* lost. No loss of territory, no disasters in other campaigns, can deprive us of the glory of that battle. That, at least, is our own. Why should we give up what was so hardly earned—what the

great and the good deem so precious ?   The glory
of that battle is our own.   It shall shame our
posterity if they degenerate !   It shall warm them
if they emulate our valour !   The English heart
is cold which forgets to glow at the recollection of
that day—when the dauntless Englishman beat
down the crest of his gigantic foe, tore the scarf
from his neck, struck the sword from his hand,
and drove him ignominiously from the field.

In passing through Poictiers, my heart exulted
not the less because that city now owned the sway .
of the sovereign of France ;   neither could the
future masters of Talavera have any control
over the trophies we carried thence.   The hand
of the spoiler may fell the fruitful olives that
shadow the graves of our fallen heroes ; but the
laurels he cannot touch.   In spite of waste, ruin,
and desolation, which follow in the train of tyrants,
unfading laurels shall grow and thicken over that
hallowed spot where English blood flowed as a
barrier against merciless oppression.

But, though no doubt can reasonably be entertained as to the victory, which is matter of fact, in
regard to the military skill evinced by the opposing
leaders there is certainly room for diversity of
opinion, governed by the supposititious results of
different measures on one part and the other.   If
we were to suppose that Lord Wellington (then
Sir Arthur Wellesley) knew the amount and con-

dition of the force under Soult, he must be a hardy partisan who would attempt to justify his conduct. In Spain, however, it is often not only impossible to procure correct information, but also extremely difficult to guard against that which is false. The Spaniards are deaf to bad news, and idiotically credulous to all reports that tend to flatter their hopes. I shall suppose that Lord Wellington's information was in accord with the general report, and stated that the French in Galicia were surrounded by patriot armies which were gradually effecting their destruction. This intelligence was corroborated, as well by the nature of Soult's retreat from Oporto as by the events which actually followed that ruinous movement. Such, indeed, were the dangers that assailed the French Marshals in Galicia, Soult and Ney, that a staff officer assured me that they both at different times merely refrained from laying down their arms because they considered such a measure more terrible than destruction itself. Besides, the personal hatred subsisting between those chiefs rankled to such a degree as often to prevent their co-operation and to urge them to deceive each other as to their intended movements. Their animosity originated in Prussia, and the troops they commanded were infected with its venom. Some curious facts about those two Frenchmen have come to my knowledge, and I shall make no excuse for introducing them here.

When Soult had effected his retreat from
Portugal by passing the Minko at Orense, after a
serious struggle with a Spanish force, he moved
upon Lugo, where Marshal Ney was maintaining
himself against the multiform enemies that goaded
him on all sides.   On arriving at Lugo, Soult
immediately repaired to the quarters of his brother
Marshal, and was ushered in by the officer who is
my informant.   From the ante-room that officer
could distinctly overhear the altercation produced
by their meeting.   On entering the room where
Ney was, Soult, after the manner of the French,
went forward with open arms to embrace him.

"Stand back," said Ney.   "I don't know you.
Where do you come from?   You come flying,
like a coward, from the enemies of the Emperor!"

"*Allons donc*," returned Soult.   "I come to
save Lugo, which you were on the point of losing."

"I neither want assistance," said the other,
"nor are you in a condition to give me any.   I
have met by hundreds your straggling fugitives.
They all had abandoned their arms, that they
might fly the faster; but their packs, heavy with
plunder, were religiously preserved!   It is you,
Monsieur le Maréchal, who have taught them to
throw away their muskets in order that they might
carry the more booty, when your orderly book
gave up such a town as Oporto to a three-days'
pillage.   Is that the way, sir, you consult your

master's interests ? To give up the second city of the country, you take in his name to the horrible excesses of your brutal soldiers ! You are no longer a Marshal of France. I will no longer acknowledge you as a chief in authority under the Emperor."

Soult, though the senior, still endeavoured to appease Ney by representing the importance of their unanimity ; but Ney was inflexible, and became so grossly abusive that Soult, unable any longer to command his temper, retorted some very harsh expressions upon the aggressor ; stung by which, that furious Marshal, suddenly drawing his sword, said, "Villain, defend thyself"—a mandate which was instantly obeyed.

As both were expert swordsmen, they contended for some time without bloodshed, and General Maurice Mathieu, rushing into the room, found them hotly engaged. Having parted them, he reported that their respective corps were volleying at each other in the great square, thus, as if by sympathy, following the example of their chiefs. This intelligence restored Ney to his senses, and both combatants, galloping into the square, by their personal efforts ended the fray of the soldiery, and quelled a civil broil of an aspect the most menacing and alarming. Some appearance of harmony was established between the Marshals ; but it was deceptive.

The abandonment of Galicia having been fixed upon between them, it was agreed that Soult should go before, and keep up a constant communication and co-operation with Ney.   No sooner had he, by his reconciliation with that haughty chieftain, reorganised and refitted his corps, than he stole a march upon him—allowing a Spanish force to take possession of a bridge between him and his colleague, by which treacherous conduct Ney was for some time isolated, expecting nothing better than destruction.

In this account, given to me by an intelligent officer, I have not attempted to supply any deficiency of particulars, even by the most probable conjectures as to times and places ; this, in order that I might withdraw myself from any stake in its authenticity.   I give it from memory, as nearly as I can in the words of my informant, and only add that he could not have the smallest motive to deceive me, and that I am well persuaded he had as little inclination to do so.   Perhaps it may be difficult to believe that two officers, high in the trust of their Sovereign, should let private hatred so completely take the place of public spirit ; yet when the temper of Soult is considered, along with the insult and defiance he met with from his inferior officer, the motives to revenge will not appear trifling ; nor is it out of nature that he should go fearful lengths to effect the ruin of his enemy.   Be

that as it may, we have seen enough to account for
the ideas of Soult's distress, which prevailed so
much in the British army as to prevent the inter-
vention of his force from being sufficiently adverted
to.   It is no wonder that, passing through the
mouths of the sanguine Spaniards, probability,
grounded on real disasters, should assume the form
of fact, and that those who saw the ship strike on
a rock should boldly assert that she went to the
bottom.

Thus the rashness of Lord Wellington in
placing himself between two enemies, the least
of whom was equal to himself, may be palliated.
His conduct, when he was in the scrape, it seems
hardly possible to find fault with.   His position
was skilfully chosen and bravely defended ; and
the resolution to head back and attack Soult,
leaving the Spaniards to check an army which he
himself had routed, was truly that of a soldier-like
spirit, and does him honour.   He could not control the event which obliged him to relinquish that
daring purpose.   He had no alternative when
General Cuesta abandoned Talavera.

On the other hand, the conduct of the French
is not so easily accounted for.   One would indeed
rather suppose that they were as much deceived as
the English respecting the corps under the three
Marshals, than that they were acting in concert with
that force.   King Joseph was so sure that his

opponent must either retreat before him or be
destroyed, that no consideration should have induced him to give battle until he knew that his
blows would be seconded in the rear of his enemy;
but flying before him when he would follow, and
following when he would recede, Joseph should
merely have kept himself in contact with the enemy
—sure that if the enemy were not to be caught, his
retreat and passage of a river, in face of a superior
force, must be ruinous in the extreme. To the power
of jealousy between the holders of delegated authority, and to that saucy confidence which has been the
stumbling-block of most of the French Generals
who have contended with us single-handed, may be
imputed the folly of Marshal Victor in urging the
King to give battle at Talavera. Nor was more
skill displayed in executing that determination than
judgment in adopting it. When a strong position
is defended by brave troops, no good General would
think of attacking it in front until every method
to turn it had been tried. The French leader did
endeavour to turn the British by the left. This
his opponent frustrated by the sacrifice of a body
of cavalry. Then the Frenchman attacked in
front, with such perseverance and with such a
weight of superior forces that all the strength of
the ground, and all the valour that defended it,
were only sufficient to repulse him. He seems to
have forgotten that there was a right flank also,

which formed the longest part of the line of
defence, and was occupied by raw, undisciplined
troops, destitute of competent officers and of that
experience in war which communicates confidence ;
that the ground they stood on, though much intersected, was easily assailable ; and that this flank
was, equally with the other, a key to the position
of his enemy.   If that night attack which he so
unwisely directed upon us had been made upon the
Spaniards, while he occupied us by a formidable
feint (for which purpose he had abundance of
troops), he would have had the fairest prospect of
success.   With the Spaniards the panic fright
attending unseen danger would have done much.
They are individually brave ; but the mass was
unknowing, and confusion would have been tanta-
mount to defeat.

I am convinced that the town of Talavera might
have been taken by 20,000 men, while 25,000
could have occupied the British in the heights.
Thus Lord Wellington must either have changed
his position with precipitation, while pressed by a
superior force, or have suffered the enemy to cut
him off from the Tagus and approach him from
the rear.   On the other hand, in attacking us
fairly in front, the enemy had no right to expect
anything but hard knocks.   He knew of old that
we should fight to the last, and had nothing to
hope from ignorance or fear.   The actual results

he ought to have anticipated. He was so completely routed (I have been behind the scenes) that, had not Soult given us check, we should inevitably have destroyed him. For seven leagues the beaten army fled in confusion. No corps, no regiment, was together. All was disorganised that had been engaged ; and the King, taking a large escort from the reserve that had been held back in case of disaster, entered Madrid a despairing fugitive.

To the egregious folly of that *soi-disant* Monarch, or of his advisers, Lord Wellington owes the occasion of success, and the army and the nation an inestimable wreath of glory.

Soldiers on the March.

CHAPTER IV

THE repulse and flight of the French restored confidence to the fugitive inhabitants. Leaving the mountains, whither they had repaired for refuge, they began to re-enter the town. Thus the house to which I had been carried had received an addition to its inmates conducing much to my comfort, since both old and young, emulous in their attentions, strove to anticipate my wants and alleviate my sufferings. The Spanish Commissary-General was received into the house as an old friend and patron. His lady was careful to supply me with the whitest bread, often coming to take a melancholy look at me, always retiring with a shake of the head and an avowed conviction that I should die.

But the evacuation of the town by the British soon repelled the returning confidence of its inhabitants, and their fears awoke with aggravated force. Don Manoel di Monton, the master of my house, again sought shelter in the mountains; but with perpetual thankfulness let me record that a

British officer, wounded and mutilated, was to the
women of the house too sacred an object to be
abandoned ; dreadful indeed as were the thoughts
of the French, the fear of them gave way to compassion. They had clung to the hope that at least
their countrymen would stay and protect them ;
but on the 4th, seeing them also file under their
windows in a long receding array, they came to me,
beating their breasts and tearing their hair, and
demanded of me if I knew what was to become of
them. Though I could not avoid being agitated
by their distress, as well as by my own situation, I
summoned my philosophy and communicated it to
them as well as I was able.

"Perhaps," said I, "you are mistaken in the
movements of our troops, or, at the worst, if the
French come now they will enter the town peaceably and commit no excesses."

The Commissary's wife, ready for departure,
came up to take leave of me and to bring me a
supply of bread, feeling that by and by it might be
difficult, perhaps impossible, to procure it. She
left the house, still exclaiming, "Ah! your poor
young Englishman will die!" Señora Pollonia,
having observed that I did not despond, expressed
considerable hopes of my recovery.

I had sent Aaron on a message to the officer
who had been left Commandant by General Wellesley. He returned presently, saying that the

Colonel was gone, having given orders throughout
the town that those in the hospitals who were able
to move should set off instantly for Oropesa, as the
French were at hand.   The sensation this notice
produced is beyond all description.   I lay perfectly
still.   I had made up my mind that it would be
better to fall into the enemy's hands than attempt
to go away.   Other men in situations like my own
had themselves placed across horses and mules,
and fruitlessly attempted to escape.   The road to
Oropesa was covered with our poor, wounded,
limping, bloodless soldiers.   On crutches or sticks,
with blankets thrown over them, they hobbled
woefully along.   For the moment panic terror
lent them a force inconsistent with their debility,
their fresh wounds, and their recent amputations.
Some lay down on the road to take their last
sleep.   The rest, unable to get farther than
Oropesa, fell afterwards into the hands of the
French, when their troops entered that town.

Such tidings, always painted to the utmost by
the apprehensive Aaron, and discoloured by the
despair of my Spanish attendants, impaired my
tranquillity.   I was sensible that, weak and exhausted as I was, my notions and expressions of
things had great influence both with the Spanish
women and with my own servants, who, I feared,
did they discover anything like alarm upon my
countenance, might consider the case desperate and

consult their own safety.   Therefore I explained
to Aaron that if the French should come my plight
would be a sure recommendation to their respect;
that he must know it would be useless to take
prisoner one who had lost a leg; and that they
would surely leave me my servant, if for no other
reason than to save themselves the trouble of providing attendance.   In using that method to re-
assure him, I spoke strictly as I believed; nor had
I the smallest idea that I should ever be moved a
prisoner from the spot.

Still, my mind was far from being at ease.   I
thought it possible that some foraging party might
plunder me and commit excesses in the house, or
on the women, who would run to me for protection
(however uselessly); nor could I, I am persuaded
(however little able to stir), have lain a passive
spectator of any violence that brutality might have
offered them.

Besides, the panic terror that had been communicated to the hospitals might, I thought, extend
to the surgeons, whose assistance was of more importance to me than any other consideration.

The evening of the 4th, however, closed in
quietness uninterrupted by the French; and I had
a visit from the senior medical officer, Mr. Higgins,
which gave me great comfort, as his conversation
taught me to confide in his conduct.

CHAPTER V

FROM the stillness which surrounded Talavera, when the morning of the 5th of August dawned upon her towers, her hills, her fields, and her olive woods, a traveller might have supposed her in profound peace, until, gazing on her gory heights, he saw that they yet streamed with blood and were covered with ghastly slain. Those horrid heaps, and the subdued moan sent forth from her hospitals, would, like the prostrate oaks of the forest, and the distant murmurs of the fallen blast, have carried to his mind some image of the storm.

The interval of tranquillity, short as it was, I employed in laying in a stock of provisions. I had a well-founded anxiety on this head, and more foresight than Pedro, who was astonished at my eagerness and extravagance.

"But, signore, the Brencone asks a dollar a couple for his chickens!"

"Buy! buy! buy!" was all the answer he could get from me.

I laid in wine, eggs, and various other provender,

at a rate equally provoking the rage and remonstrance of the little Italian. About the middle of the day, a violent running and crying under my windows announced an alarm. The women rushed into my room, exclaiming, "Los Franceses! los Franceses!"

The assistant surgeon of Artillery came in.

"Well, Mr. Staniland," said I, "are the French coming?"

"Yes," he answered : "I believe so."

"Where is Mr. Higgins?"

"He is gone out to meet them."

"That's right," said I.

In about an hour, however, Mr. Higgins entered, saying, "I have been out of town above two leagues, and can see nothing of them. If, however, they do come, they will have every reason to treat us with attention ; for they will find their own wounded lying alongside of ours, provided with the same comforts, treated with the same care. I have been completely round myself, to see that the treatment of their officers and men was in every respect upon the same footing as our own, so that they will have no possible pretext for complaint ; and I can boldly claim their protection and respect. Whenever they come, I shall meet them and solicit the General to visit the hospitals with me."

In the course of this day Mr. Staniland brought me messages of condolence from my friend Captain

Taylor of the Artillery, who was severely wounded by a grape shot in the groin. His wound was not considered dangerous; but his spirits were miserably depressed at the thought of being left behind. He sent me a project for our joint removal, as soon as we should be well enough to follow our army; and I, though well convinced that the French would very shortly enter the town, willingly allowed myself to be cheated, and my thoughts to be turned in that cheering direction.

The 5th of August closed upon the renovated hopes of the unhappy people of Talavera; their feelings made a rapid transition from despair to security; and they laid down their heads in peace.

On the 6th, reports of the enemy's approach were treated with total disregard. Between eight and nine the galloping of horses was heard in the street. The women ran to the windows, and instantly shrank back, pale as death, with each a finger on her lips in token of silence. "Los demonios!" they whispered; and then cautiously watched, on tiptoes and aside, in breathless expectation of some bloody scene.

"They have swords and pistols all ready," said Manoela, trembling.

"How's this?" cried old Pollonia. "Why, they pass the English soldiers, unnoticed! And see there—they go talking and laughing together! Jesus! Maria! what's all this?"

" Jesus ! " cries Manoela.

" Maria ! " adds Catalina.

" Jose ! " concludes old Pepa.

In short, nothing could exceed their astonishment at that display of civilised warfare ; and I had scarce yet persuaded them to believe their senses when Mr. Higgins again made his appearance.

He had ridden out to meet the General who commanded the cavalry, and on making the representation he had preconcerted, had found that soldier prodigal of encomiums, assurances, and professions.

" The chance of war," said he to Higgins, " has thrown your unfortunate countrymen into the power of the French, who will be incapable of abusing it. If respect for the bravery of our adversaries and the dictates of humanity could ever be disregarded by us, gratitude for the manner in which now and on every occasion you have treated us, when the same chance of war has thrown us into your power, would make it impossible for us to consider these unhappy Englishmen otherwise than as the most sacred trust to our national generosity. And as for you medical gentlemen, who have been humane and manly enough not to desert your duty to your patients (many of whom are Frenchmen) in the hour of difficulty and distress, and have done us the honour to trust yourselves in our hands, not

the smallest constraint will be put upon your
motions. Stay amongst us as long as you please ;
go when you will. You are as free as the air you
breathe. And whenever you think proper, our
safe-conduct and unfeigned thanks shall attend you
to your countrymen."

We had afterwards reason enough to know how
much we were indebted to this good beginning
arranged by Mr. Higgins. Only their wish to
support some appearance of consistency checked
their natural disposition to ill-treat us.

Throughout, Mr. Higgins displayed the character of no common man. To be loaded with the
charge of such groaning multitudes — almost
wholly unprovided with medicines, medical stores,
or provisions—would have been regarded by most
medical men as a task of no common ardour ; and
to perform it at the expense of personal liberty and
all prospects of advancement was a case of peculiar
hardship. But to prepare for the approaching
crisis,—determined to ride forth and parley with
the enemy, and persuade him that he owes you
respect, gratitude,—this is the province of an
officer of.the first class ; and Mr. Higgins in so
acting—in adopting the duties of every station that
happened to be vacant, in letting no office stop for
want of an officer, but supplying the place of the
absent, and encouraging the present—discovered
a manly superiority, a dauntless indifference to

events, that communicated confidence through
every inferior branch and secured to his suffering
countrymen the blessings of a perfect medical attendance and the protection and respect of their
enemies.

MANOELA   TIA MARIA   TIA PEPA (p. 110).

CHAPTER VI

THE party that had first entered the town, having found no resistance, had no sooner established their quarters and disposed of their horses than they addressed themselves to the purposes of plunder; and various reports reached us, sufficient to overset the confidence which Mr. Higgins's account had inspired. Yet when Mr. Staniland came and related several instances of the respect and distinction preserved by those marauders towards British officers, the agitated women began to hope that their dwelling would, on my account, be exempt from the horrors of pillage. Too soon, however, every hope gave place to the consciousness of contiguous danger; for again Mr. Staniland appeared, and again related to us passing events; and this time they were ominously fearful.

Three troopers, he said, had entered the quarters of my poor friend Taylor, and, coming into the room where he lay, began with the most perfect *sang froid* to rifle his portmanteau. Taylor stormed, and told them he was an English captain. "Major, 'tis very possible," said they; "but your money, your watch, and your linen are never the worse for that!" "No; nor your bread, nor your wine!" added another; and with those words the ruthless savage swallowed the wine and pocketed the bread that had been portioned out to the languishing sufferer as his sustenance and comfort for that day. In short, in spite of his remonstrances, having obliged him to deliver up all the money he had—in search of which they ransacked the very bed and mattresses on which he was stretched—having taken his watch (which was of value) and all his linen (which was invaluable), and having devoured his daily bread, they left him, expressing the coolest contempt at his feeble menaces.

Feeling that such might be my case, still, even while Taylor continued to speak, I instantly took measures to conceal whatever was most valuable to me; and having deposited my money in a little earthen vessel, I sent it to be buried in the yard, and my watch and a great jar of wine to be otherwise concealed. Then, calling for my soup, which was at the fire, and hastily dispatching it, I poured into a large glass the last of General Sherbrooke's claret, and drank it with a sort of spiteful defiance, saying to myself, "You don't get this, my boys!"

Nothing that was at all less than the coil itself could be worse than the expectation of it into which Mr. Staniland's story threw me. Every object that I had been trying to consider a comfort in my distress, I no longer dare expect to be allowed the enjoyment of. The neatness and propriety that had been preserved about my bed now only served to mortify me, and to make the expected ransack the more cruel. The quiescence of spirit so desirable for one in my state was driven away. I took a mental leave of all that I could not hide, and began to consider how the money I had buried would renew that quiescence when the storm should have ceased.

When Mr. Staniland paid his visit next morning, he told us that the French infantry would arrive in an hour, and that the town was to be given up to pillage, because deserted by the inhabitants ; "and," he added, "I am told that the General says it is impossible to put a guard over every British officer, and that they must take their chance with the rest. So I have had Captain Taylor removed to the hospital, where he will be safe."

The women consulted me on the propriety of locking the street door. "By all means," said I. "Make it as fast as you can, and don't show yourselves at the windows." The room where I lay looked into the street over the principal door, so that all parleys with the enemy must necessarily be held from my room.

Soon we heard the music playing before the infantry as it entered the town, and the women came flocking to the windows as if to see a raree-show, forgetting, in their eagerness for sights and songs, that these only announced the approach of the most wasteful ruin.

The soldiers marched close under my windows, passing through the town, to be encamped without the walls.

Soon after *thump! thump! thump!* sounded at the door. "Virgin of my soul!" said old Pollonia, tottering to the window. "There they are!" But, peeping out cautiously, she exclaimed, "No! 'tis but a neighbour. Open the door, Pepa."

"You had better," said I, "for the present, not suffer your door to be opened at all."

"No, no!" returned Pollonia; but Pepa pulled the string, and in came the neighbour.

"Well, neighbour, what news?"

"Jesus! Maria!" she exclaimed in a shrill tone. "The demons are breaking open every door, and plundering every house — all the goods — bales, chests — everything — dragged out into the street!"

"Maria di mi alma! Señora!'

"Dios santissimo!"

"Jesus!"

The crashing of doors, the tearing of windows,

loud thumpings, knockings, and clatterings were now distinctly heard in every direction ; and all outside seemed to boil in turmoil.

Ere long *thump! thump!* at our own door.

"Jesus! Maria! Jose!" the women screamed. But it was only another neighbour : so Pepa drew the string, and in the neighbour came, carrying the furniture of her house. Her head was piled up to a prodigious height with mattresses, blankets, quilts, and pillows. Under one arm were gowns, petticoats, caps, bonnets, and ribands, snatched up in the confusion of haste ; her other hand held a child's chair, and strange articles of rude hardware seemingly but little worth the fervent anxiety which her countenance betrayed for their preservation. Add to all this that her figure was of a stunted and ludicrous character, and that she came in abruptly with a doleful crying face, under that cumbrous weight of household furniture, and beginning a dismal whine. All the grievances of my fellows in misfortune, heaped upon mine, could not suppress my laughter when that strange little figure burst upon my view.

"For the love of God, señora !" she said, "let me put these mattresses in your house."

"Woman," exclaimed Pollonia, "how is my house safer than your own?"

"O, señora, for the love of God ! for the love of God!"

This pathetic adjuration was irresistible : they showed the good woman up into the garret.

Her example was followed by so many, that I feared the French would be enticed to the house. I told Doña Pollonia so ; but she did not mind me. "Yes, yes, señor," she said, and then pulled the string again.

But soon there was a loud knocking at the door, accompanied by a volley of French oaths, that left me no doubt as to the nature of this disturbance. The door was assailed with such vehemence that it shook the house. Fearing that it could not resist much longer, I endeavoured to make a diversion from the window.

Summoning Pedro the Italian, who had a few words of barbarous French, "Tell them, Pedro," said I, "that this is the quarter of an English captain."

Pedro, who, when I took him at Coimbra, had totally lost his wits, and was naturally a poor, pusillanimous, miserable devil, had yet a little degree of Italian sharpness and education about him. He cautiously approached the window, and peeped out in breathless agitation.

"Gad so ! there is but one," said he, somewhat assured, "and he has no arms. Hallo ! sair—la maison for Inglis captin ! Go to hell ! "

Though much harassed and annoyed, this per- fection in language, and the abrupt jabbering way in which it was delivered, forced the laughter out of me.

"Ouvrez la porte — bête!" vociferated the Frenchman, "I want some water," and again he banged the door.

"Holy Virgin!" said Pollonia. "We had better open the door!"

"No! no! no!" cried I. "Tell him, Pedro, that if he does not take himself off I shall send and report him to the General."

Pedro began in the same heterogeneous dialect to deliver my message; but he had not got half through it, when suddenly he ducked his head lower than his knees, and a great stone, whirling through the space he had vacated, struck the opposite wall.

"Il demonio!" muttered the women, as they ducked their heads.

Here, however, when the siege seemed most likely to prevail, it was unexpectedly raised; for the fellow, who was drunk, finding we would not open the door, and that he would get nothing but Pedro's jabber, just banged a stone at his head, and reeled off in search of some easier adventure.

CHAPTER VII

Pedro had hardly time to congratulate himself on his victory before the portal was again assailed.

"O!" said Pollonia, "it's only two officers' servants"; and she entered into conversation with them awhile, and then shut the window.

"Well," said I, "what did the officers' servants want?"

"They wanted lodging for their masters; but I told them you were here, and that we had no room."

"And have you room?"

"Yes—but I didn't choose to say so."

"Run, Pedro," cried I,—"run and tell those servants that there is excellent accommodation here, both for their masters and for their horses. Persuade them to come if you possibly can! Don't you perceive, señora, that this is the only chance for preserving your house from pillage?"

But even this consideration could hardly reconcile the old lady to receive *los demonios* as lodgers in her house without having done her utmost to keep them out.

The two servants were far from unwilling to return. I sent for one of them—a Prussian lad of about thirteen. He spoke French very ill, but enough to tell me that he was servant to Captain de la Platière, who was aide-de-camp to the General of Division Villatte. The other lad, he said, was servant to his master's comrade, who held a similar situation under the same General.

I had seen enough of the French military to know that it was uncertain whether the falling into the hands of two French officers would be a mercy or a misfortune. A class so large must contain extremes of good and bad; and when education, habits, and example balanced the wrong way, it was evident on which side the scale must preponderate. Notwithstanding all this, the hope that my fellow-lodgers would prove gentlemen encouraged a momentary feeling of security, and I anxiously wished for their arrival.

Meantime little Pedro observed the motions of the two servant lads with the eye of a lynx.

"Signore," said he, "those two *diavoli* are prying about into every hole and corner. I fear me they suspect something is hid."

Though I did not think there could be any truth in his conjecture, I sent Aaron to dig up my money, and bring my watch and the wine upstairs.

Soon after in came Pedro, strutting with a most consequential air.

"The French Captain, sir!" said he.

There followed him a fine, military‑looking figure, of a frank countenance, carried erect—with his hat on—armed *cap-à-pie*, and covered with martial dust.

He advanced to my bedside with a quick step, and a great air of frankness and anxiety.

"I have had the misfortune, sir, to lose a limb," said I, "and I claim your protection."

"My protection!" answered he, putting out his hand. "Command my devoted services! The name of an Englishman in distress is sufficient to call forth our most tender attention. Assuredly a wounded man can have no enemy; but the wounded of a nation so merciful to its fallen enemies have the most pressing claim upon our gentleness and friendship. 'Tis no favour—'tis our positive duty—to treat you with the same generosity and humanity which in our reverses we ever experience from you. We love and respect the English character, though our governments are always hostile. Compose yourself, my friend : you can receive nothing from the French but the alleviating care which your pitiable situation demands."

I was a good deal affected by the kindness of this speech. What he said was very true ; but it

was particularly delicate and acceptable to say it
now. Kindness can never be thoroughly felt
unless it be greatly wanted. Then it makes an
indelible impression.

After sitting with me a few minutes (during
which, in the most friendly manner, he inquired
into all my wants), this gracious enemy prepared
to leave me. Upon which I begged that occasionally, as he found leisure, he would pay me a visit,
as I should consider a few moments' chat now and
then a great relief.

" I will not only come myself," said he, " but I
will bring my companion with me, who will be at
least as solicitous as myself to soften a little the
rigour of your situation."

So he left me, much more comfortable than he
found me. My roast pigeon was served up in
security : half of it, and a little bottle of wine,
I sent to Taylor, who (poor fellow) was extremely
well pleased with the present.

Señora Pollonia was charmed with the Captain's
kind manner to me ; said he was very good,
though a Frenchman, and that (she now remembered) he had lodged with her, when the
French were last in the town, and had never
offended her — but that the servants were sad
pigarones.

Towards evening M. de la Platière brought in
his companion, Captain Simon, whose appearance

was still more prepossessing. He had the advantage of extreme youth, and was remarkably good-looking.

His manners could not be more kind than those of the other ; but they were more soft and insinuating — his attention was more quiet and more delicate. He came and sat by my bed, and found many little things to say that might be consoling and inspiriting.

At the capture of the French at St. Domingo he was with Rochambaud, and might have been in England till now, but that he was befriended by Sir Thomas Duckworth, because he was high in the honours of freemasonry. The British merchants at Jamaica had treated him with hospitality fervid as their sun, and their generous presents had supplied him with a sumptuous sea stock for his voyage to England.

Thus he had received a most favourable impression of English character and English society. He knew some words of English, and with a tempered vivacity found means to make his conversation consolatory and agreeable.

Both offered to procure me dinner from their General's table. They went out on purpose to borrow books for me, and brought me some volumes, highly productive of resource for many weeks. They complimented me upon the valour and conduct of the British troops, and declared they had never witnessed a carnage so dreadful, or a battle so bravely contested.

In short, these officers did everything that men ought to do amid such circumstances ; besides which, their personal qualifications and sprightly ease and candour of behaviour made me indebted to them for an alleviation which many with dispositions equally good would not have had it in their power to afford.

Thus was my situation for the moment even amended by captivity ; and I regained the calm of spirit necessary to my recovery.

The Fellow I saw on the Spire.

CHAPTER VIII

IT was not long that I was permitted to enjoy the alleviation which the society of those good-natured officers afforded me. On the 7th they apprised me that the Division of Villatte was about to move, and that they must take their leave of me that night : before daybreak they must depart.

A rough cavalry officer bore them company in my room ; he had long moustaches, was black, and looked a ruffian. They discoursed of England and France, and disputed on the present grandeur and future policy of the Emperor. Their opposite ideas bore no stamp of originality. It seemed as if they were reciting the current and popular language of the society in which they lived, rather than stating genuine opinions, the result of individual reflection.

It has been remarked that the French think less than other people, and that they are more liable than others to a contagion of sentiment, which, though it may render their conversation insipid to themselves, enables a foreigner the more readily to ascertain the general disposition. Conversing with one, you have the sentiments of a multitude! Yet these officers possessed a rapidity of utterance, propriety of language, and fire of gesture very like eloquence. Simon had a breadth in his cadence peculiar to the natives of Blois; that of de la Platière was impoverished by the refinement of Paris. Both spoke with a fluency and precision astonishing to an Englishman; and the Moustache interposed his barbarous sentiments with gruff and ferocious bluntness.

"The Emperor," said de la Platière, "may pretend to wish for peace, but it cannot be true. He is a warrior, and his element is a career of daring enterprise. His ambition is insatiate; he can't live beneath a serene heaven. It must be troubled with thunder and dark clouds, which he gilds and empurples by the glory of his achievements. I do not indeed believe that the conquest of England forms any part of his design—he knows too much to hope it. But, on the other hand, what has he to fear from her that he should wish for peace, notwithstanding his love of war?"

"Mais, mon Dieu," exclaimed Simon, "after the feats he has performed—after having led the French through a track of conquest unprecedentedly splendid—after being to France a tutelary genius and an avenging deity—subjugating her enemies

without—within replacing her laws, re-establishing
her religion, multiplying her manufactures, beauti-
fying her cities—and recalling the arts and sciences
to their forsaken haunts—is it not most natural
that the hero should at length incline to repose
beneath the luxuriant shade of so many laurels ;
that he should now seek to consolidate and secure
the vast dominion he has attained ; to cure the
populace of the disease of conscription ; to nurse
and recover the vigour of his finances, by stopping
the vast flow from his widely-wasted treasures ; and
to reward the fidelity and bravery of his followers
by conferring on them the blessings of property
and peace ? But he cannot attain these desirable
objects any other way than by a strict alliance and
treaty of commerce with England—with no other
power ! If Napoleon and George the Third
would but say, ' Eh ! soyons amis ! Let us divide
the world between us—take you the seas, the
islands, and the colonies, and I will take continental
Europe '—no sooner said than done ! "

" Augh ! C'est clair," exclaimed de la Platière ;
" and I wish with all my heart it was so ! Messieurs
les Anglais would then give us many things which
we cannot do too well without, and we should
send them wines of Bordeaux and Champagne.
We should go to amuse ourselves in London, and
they should return with us to Paris ; and all the
world could go and come at their ease."

"Mais imaginez-vous, mon cher," continued Simon, "la grandeur, la puissance alors de ces deux nations! Augh! They are actually the only two nations upon earth! They contend without materially affecting the safety or the power of each other. The little states are not safe within the wind of such commotion; but the belligerents are too equally matched to gain anything by war. If serious hurt be done, it acts on both. Both may be weakened by loss of blood, but the superiority remains as undecided as ever."

"Those," interrupted Moustache, "are the speculations of politicians. All I know is that if I were the Emperor I would burn every house and cut the throat of every human being on the continent of Spain! These miserable dogs of Spaniards, that murder and torture us whenever they can catch us straggling or sick! Pardi! I would make a fire in Spain of which the people in England should see the light, and know with what a signal vengeance we visit those who dare to maltreat the soldiers of France!"

"Well," said Simon, visibly shocked at this burst of tigerism, "let us talk no more of these matters, for I fear we fatigue this poor Captain!"

"Ay," said de la Platière. "We had better leave him; it cannot be good for him to talk so much! [I had scarce spoken.] Good-night, my

friend.   We shall soon return, and we hope to improve our acquaintance ! "

"In the meantime," added Simon, "we have
spoken of you in the most pressing manner to the
officer who remains here as Commandant de la
Place.   His name is de Bon, and he is an excellent man.   If you should want anything, and
send to him, he will render you every service in
his power.   Adieu ! "

I was truly sorry to part with these two officers,
not only because they had interested me by their
kindness, but also because, when they were gone, I
should no longer have any security from the
licentious visits of lounging soldiers ; of which
possibility they themselves were sensible, for they
recommended me to conceal my money ; and
de la Platière wrote his name upon the door,
in the hope that it might discourage those from
entering whose purposes would not bear the
scrutiny of their superiors.

Whether this frequent vicissitude of unquiet-
ness were the cause, or whether it arose from the
natural progress of cure, I know not ; but I now
became subject to severe and almost incessant
pain—the more harassing, as I could not seek to
alleviate it by the slightest change of position,
a relief which could not be attempted without
risking serious consequences.

This, indeed, had been a harassing day.   My

5

fancied security had fallen from under me at a time when bodily pain began to tincture with discouragement the excursions of the mind ; and I was vexed and disturbed by disagreeable reports of disasters to the British, and rigidly confined to one position, from the long continuance in which my whole frame had become irritable and uneasy.

To this apparently irremediable extremity the influence of opium applied a sweet and almost magical assuasive. I swallowed two little pills, and in half an hour how changed was my state! Every throb of anguish was profoundly stilled! Awake, I had only the consciousness of inviolable repose. Every sound was hushed. The voices in the room, or the noises in the street, though heard, were disarmed of all power to disturb my rest. The mind, still at liberty, and only disposed to range over the most peaceful and soothing scenes, restored me to my family, softly weeping with tender gladness at my return. So wondrous did it seem to be snatched from such wretchedness and placed in such measureless and enchanted repose, a line of Milton kept playing softly upon the ear of my understanding :

> Yet with a pleasing sorcery could charm
> Pain for awhile—and anguish . . .

Yet with a pleasing sorcery could charm pain for awhile ! Then came the sweetly solemn, composed,

and grave numbers of Milton, loosely floating
on my mind with the gentlest recurrence :

> The song was partial—but the harmony
> (What could it less, when spirits immortal sing)
> Suspended Hell, and took with ravishment
> The thronged audience . . .

Most grateful is the remembrance of these charmed
moments—indelible their sweet impression.

I have written the account of them with a
fidelity that to some will compensate for its seeming incoherency, and they who think I rave will
find me brought to my senses in the next chapter.

Bridge of Alcantara (p. 215).

CHAPTER IX

Thus entranced, and while conscious that the stillness of night had not yet given place to the busy
hum of day, I was suddenly roused by the unwelcome accents of Moustache.

"Eh, Capitaine, comment se va-t-il? se va
mieux! Hah! bon!"

When he had brought me down from the fairy
voyage I was engaged in, he showed me that the
blade of his sword was broken, and that it was
no longer serviceable to give the soldiers the *coup
plat de sabre*.

"As prisoner of war," said he, "you will have
no use for a sword. Give me yours, and if you
will, keep mine. 'Tis as good for you—as any!
Where is your sword?"

"It stands," said I, "in yonder corner. Take
it, by all means."

"Ha! bon!" returned he. "Je vous laisserai
la mienne."

So saying and so doing, he brushed off.

For my sword I did not care. He had said

truly that I should have no use for it ; but to be
disturbed from a gentle rest was to one in my
state a serious annoyance ; and to be called from a
rest whose soothing dream was Liberty by a hoarse
voice croaking " Prisoner of War ! " was exasper-
ating.   I am afraid I wished the sword in his
gizzard ; and from that moment my hopes of
exemption from captivity were broken.

When dark Catalina came with my breakfast,
she informed me that the bread I then saw was the
last, and that the bakers were prohibited from
selling any.   Upon this I sent a note to the Commandant de la Place, requesting his assistance.
He soon paid me a visit, and assured me that I
should want nothing which he could supply.   He
was an elderly, respectable-looking man, and,
sitting down by me, began to talk very rationally
upon general subjects.   I told him how much I
was obliged to the kindness of the two officers
who recommended me to him, and how much I
deplored their absence.

" They are," said he, " two very amiable young
men.   You will soon see them again.   They will
probably be back to-morrow.   In the meantime, I
shall endeavour to supply their place.   Come, send
your servant with me.   I will find him some white
bread."

Saying this, he left me, having relieved my
dread of starving and of being plundered ; for

I learned from him that my two friends, in the expectation of immediate return, had left their servants, horses, and effects.

One anxiety made room for another, much more distressing—much nearer my heart—much more difficult to dismiss.

I remembered in what uncertainty as to my life the accounts that had been sent to my family would leave them, and that to this uncertainty would be added the horror of knowing that in so forlorn and helpless a condition I had been abandoned to an enemy made savage by a sanguinary war, and exasperated by recent defeat. Slender as the hope was that a letter would, amid such circumstances, reach its destination, my mind would, I thought, be easier after making the attempt.

Accordingly, I again applied to the Commandant, who referred me to General Séméllé, Chief of the Staff.

It was then too late, I thought, to intrude on the General. So, having dined, and chatted with Catalina and Mr. Higgins, until my pains began to grow wearisome, I had recourse to the wondrous medicine, and tranquil repose soon held me in her soft embrace.

Next morning, after I had breakfasted, and the surgeon had performed his office, I called for pen, ink, and paper, and wrote to my father as follows :—

TALAVERA DE LA REGNA, 9th August 1809.

My EVER DEAREST FATHER,—I would give a great deal to know that this letter will reach you soon, for its purpose is to tell you that my recovery is proceeding fast. My dressing to-day gave me no pain. My appetite is good, and my spirits would be so if it were not from the fear of what you suffer.

The French officers have treated me with the most compassionate kindness, supplying me with books, or whatever else they thought might alleviate my situation.

As soon as I can travel, I shall go to Madrid, which is only four days' easy journey from hence; and then I have great hopes of being allowed to return to England on parole—for the French do not witness misfortune unmoved, any more than the English.

Let me think, my dearest Father, that the knowledge of my situation will be a relief to your anxiety. In this world, misfortunes must be borne; if borne with patience, they diminish; it is easier for us to bear them who believe that we shall all meet at last, in a world where they have no place!

We shall lessen the weight of actual misfortune by considering how naturally it might have been heavier. If, instead of the loss of a leg, the ball had taken any of the many frightful directions that make a man an object for life, and to which my body was equally exposed; or had it passed through my head, and debarred me from you for ever, how much more need would you have had of your fortitude and resignation!

The operation promises the most favourable result. Consider then how capable I may hope to be of the enjoyment of my friends, and let me find amongst them a house of joy, not a house of mourning!

God bless you, my Mother and the rest ! And believe me ever, yours, my dearest Father, CHARLES.

Having finished this letter, I accompanied it by a note in French to General Séméllé, describing my situation and the motives which pressed upon me to give my friends some bulletin of my health.

In a very short time an officer, coming in and presenting a letter to me, announced himself as the aide-de-camp of General Séméllé. After thanking him for the honour he did me, I opened the letter and read as follows :—

A Monsieur Charles Boothby,
  Capitaine du Génie, au service de S. M. Bque.

TALAVERA, *le 9 août,* 1809.

MONSIEUR LE CAPITAINE,—J'ai reçu la lettre que vous m'avez fait l'honneur de m'adresser, et par laquelle vous me faites la demande d'envoyer à M. le Lieut.-Gal. Sherbrooke une dépêche qui a pour objet de l'instruire de l'état dans lequel vous vous trouvez, pour en donner avis à vos amis et parens en Angleterre.

Je vous assure, M. le Capitaine, que vos vœux à cet égard seront remplis, et dans l'instant même votre lettre va être envoyée aux avant-postes ennemis.

Si dans la position où vous vous trouvez, je puis vous être de quelqu'utilité, je vous prie de disposer de moi ; je saisirai avec empressement l'occasion de vous prouver combien nous sommes reconnaissans des soins et des procédés que l'armée Anglaise a eu pour nos blessés et prisonniers.—J'ai l'honneur d'être, Monsieur le Capitaine, avec une parfaite considération, votre très humble serviteur, le Gal. Chef de l'État, Major-Gal. du 1er Corps,

SÉMÉLLÉ.

Translation

To Mr. Charles Boothby, Captain of Engineers
in the Service of His Bic. Majesty.

TALAVERA, 9*th August* 1809.

SIR—I have received the letter which you have done me the honour to address to me, and by which you request me to send to Lieut.-General Sherbrooke a despatch which has for object to instruct him of the state in which you find yourself, in order to give advice of it to your friends and relations in England.

I assure you, sir, that your wishes in this respect shall be fulfilled, and even now your letter is about to be sent to the advance posts of the enemy.

If in the situation in which you find yourself I can be at all useful to you, I beg you will command me; I shall seize with eagerness the opportunity of proving to you how much we are grateful for the consideration and care which the English army has had for our wounded and prisoners.—I have the honour to be, sir, with a perfect consideration, your very humble servant, the General Chief of the Gal. Staff of the 1st Corps,

SÉMÉLLÉ.

The gracious manner of this letter was so pleasing, and its substance relieved me from such a weight, that after reading it I remained some moments overcome.

"And will you tell General Séméllé, sir," said I, turning my head towards the aide-de-camp— "will you express to him how sensibly I feel the kindness of his conduct—how much I am penetrated by the goodness of his letter ?   I am but an indifferent Frenchman—nor can I at present talk much in any language—but that so mild and so kind a man as your General will make allowance for ! "

"My General," said the aide-de-camp, "has charged me to offer his services to any extent, and has desired me to assure you that he should think it a piece of good fortune to be able in the least degree to alleviate your suffering."

He then left me inexpressibly comforted.

I could now reasonably hope that my father would be apprised of my welfare subsequently to my being prisoner. This hope relieved me so much that I almost forgot I had any evils to contend with.

In the afternoon Pedro rushed in, in great agitation, and affirmed that the General himself was below, and begged to know if I would see him.

"Beg him to come up, Pedro," said I.   And quickly he ushered in an officer of about the age of five-and-thirty.   He was splendidly dressed, of an elegant person and a finely-formed countenance, beaming with good-nature and intelligence.

He came up to where I lay, and seeing that
I received him with some emotion, without waiting for the form of salutation, instantly seated
himself in a chair that was close to my pillow;
and, laying his hand upon my arm, he said in a
very mild and agreeable voice:

"Ne vous dérangez, mon ami! Solely I am
come to see if I can possibly lighten a little the
weight of your misfortune. Tell me, I beseech
you! Can I be useful to you? Have you everything you want? Do you suffer much?"

For all these kind inquiries I expressed my gratitude more by manner than by words. I told the
General, however, that since he had given me
hopes of sending a letter to England, I really had
nothing to ask—nothing to wish for—"unless,
indeed," I added, "you could send me there
too."

"Ah! if you were able to move," said he, "I
would take it upon myself to exchange you—for
just now I have the power; but by the time you
will have gained strength enough to travel you
will be at the disposal of the Major-General of
the army."

"Good Heavens!" I exclaimed. "Could not
you make the arrangement now, to be executed
afterwards? I cannot express the joy it would
give me!"

"Ah, non!" he said; "but you have no cause

for disquiet on that score. In your situation you will meet with no difficulty. Make yourself easy!"

Then, having again entreated that I would freely apply to him if I stood in need of his assistance, and repeating many expressions of kindness and protection, he left me. The comfort I had derived from his letter was much augmented by his charitable visit.

"Caps of this sort are worn by the wealthier peasantry—as Alcaldes and such. They are made of brown cloth stiffened in the crown, and garnished with black velvet ribbons and tassels."

CHAPTER X

In the evening de la Platière and Simon returned.
We were already well acquainted, and our meet-
ing was that of old friends. After inquiries as to
how I had passed the time in their absence, de la
Platière began to inform me that Sir Arthur
Wellesley had met with disasters.

"Taisez-vous, mon cher!" interrupted Simon,
in an under voice : "it may have a bad effect on
his spirits!"

The other pulled up ; and they would have
given a sudden turn to the conversation, but that
my anxiety was awakened, and I begged to be
frankly informed of all that had happened.

"Ce n'est rien, mon cher," said Simon. "Your
General—Wellesley—finding the roads impracticable, has been obliged to leave behind him his
baggage and artillery. Qu'est ce que cela lui
fera ? En Angleterre il en trouvera d'autres ! "

"En Angleterre!" I exclaimed. "Comment
donc ? "

"Mais oui! He is making forced marches

upon Cadiz, where plait au ciel he will embark."

"Thank Heaven!" cried de la Platière. "Messieurs les Anglais once at sea, we will soon finish the campaign! Sacré dieu! nous la finirons bientôt, allez!"

"O!" said the other, "'tis the best you can do! Return to your happy island and leave us to quiet and restore this miserable country. Shed no more of your generous blood in the cause of a people unworthy of your friendship! See how they have treated you! When in their cause you have been fighting like gods, have they not tamely looked on and seen your brave soldiers fall by hundreds—nay, by thousands—without daring to make the smallest effort that might divert from your ranks the fury of the carnage? And now, when the bare thought of what you lose and what you suffer for them should tincture their valour with the noblest enthusiasm, how has this touching incentive worked on these barbarous Spaniards? They have butchered where they could their wounded enemies! And you — their wounded friends—in their cause wounded—have they not basely abandoned? They merit not what you do and what you feel for them. They are a nation of savages, who will be improved by being conquered. They are fit for nothing else."

"Poor Spaniards!" I ejaculated.

"I acknowledge," he added, "that they suffer grievous misfortunes, and I respect their determination to defend their country. But I detest them for their dark, bloody, assassinating ferocity. Dieu du Ciel! c'est horrible! I believe they would as soon murder you, their allies, if they found you alone and unprotected, as they would us."

"O pardon me," said I. "I have been all over the country alone. Every cottage—every palace—contained my friends and entertainers. So much were they impressed with gratitude for our conduct towards their country, that I received more the homage due to a superior being than the usual demonstrations of hospitality and good-will."

I suppose the Frenchmen feared, from the animation with which I spoke this, that the subject might excite efforts beyond my strength; for with one accord, giving assent to what I had said, they begged they might not make me talk more than was good for me, and the conversation relapsed into that little easy chit-chat in which I might either join or not, or join sufficiently by a smile or a monosyllable.

I showed them the letter General Séméllé had written to me.

"Il n'a fait que son devoir," said they. "O! from our wounded we have heard innumerable.

instances where your generous countrymen have
preserved them from the fury of the Spaniards.
We will endeavour not to be behindhand with
you. The King himself has declared that he will
make the wounded we have taken here his
peculiar care."

While we were talking in this manner, a French
soldier walked quietly into the room, and, coming
up to the foot of the bed, stood before the officers,
astounded, petrified. When, after sternly eyeing
him awhile, they sharply demanded his business,
his faculties returned ; and, stammering out that
he took it for a shop, he made good his retreat.
There seemed to be no doubt that his purpose was
plunder, and I congratulated myself on the protection I enjoyed. I was still suffering, still
immovable, oppressed by the excessive heat, and
tormented by innumerable flies that blackened all
the neighbourhood of my bed. Opium, patience,
and lemonade assuaged some of these evils.
Against the last, little Theresa, with a towel
fastened to the end of a long cane, was very
assiduous. Theresa was a very comical, arch little
girl, and graced her occupation by many remarks
of mingled simplicity and intelligence.

The day after my fellow-lodgers had returned,
it was known that the corps of Victor was about
to move towards the mountains of Toledo to
repress the menacing attitude of General Venegas,

who continued to threaten the Capital, and thereby to keep alive the ferment within it.

Victor was to be succeeded by Mortier in the occupancy of Talavera and its vicinity, while the united corps of Soult and Ney would show face to the allied army. My friends, in expressing their sorrow at again leaving me, assured me that the moment the troops destined to relieve them should arrive they would engage a particular friend of theirs to succeed them in their quarters. In pursuance of this promise, next day (the 11th) they brought with them a young officer of mild manners—fair in look, and strikingly gentleman-like. He said he regretted that he must decline taking the lodging proposed to him by his friends, but that should by no means impede his services to me ; and he was convinced that he could with equal certainty offer those of General Girard, commanding in Talavera, to whom he had the honour to be aide-de-camp. Recollecting the visit of the soldier who took the house for a shop, I asked if it would be possible to put a sentry in the house : the proposal was supported by my two friends, and readily assented to by the stranger. Then de la Platière and Simon took their leave, expressing the kindest wishes for my welfare ; and I, as I returned them, added one that we might meet again under better auspices. This time my sorrow at their departure was unaccompanied by

6

apprehension; nor did they leave me destitute of enlivening society.

The artillery surgeon was unremitting in his attendance, meeting Mr. Higgins at my quarters invariably at ten o'clock every morning; and their visit was usually repeated in the course of the day. As Mr. Higgins had of necessity inter-course with the French commanders, from him I used to hear all the news. His mind was of such a cheerful cast that it kept its tone amid all diffi-culties and all extremities. Never did I receive from his presence other than consolation. Since the battle he had never taken off his clothes—seldom, indeed, had rested—was ever in want of what could never be procured; and yet no whining —no complaining—no giving up!

Besides the occasional conversation of my medical attendants, I had that of the Spanish women, who, after the first emotions which patriotic feelings and domestic injuries had caused, soon regained a cheerful composure. I think that women are more excellent in this than men. We know that their feelings are more susceptible and more easily agitated; but when the blow, whatever it be, has fallen, and the inefficacy of lamentation has become evident, woman resumes her composure sooner than man. This was observable on both sides when poor Don Manoel re-entered his habitation. Gloomy and despairing was his sallow visage;

his dark beard long and neglected. While his deep-folding cloak barely concealed the disorder of his dress, his hat, which he never removed (an old slouching cocked hat), rested on his eyebrows and flapped upon either shoulder. Forgetting all other consolation save that of shrouding himself in the tawny fumes of tobacco, dismal and breathing smoke he stalked about the house with the fearful gait of muttering melancholy madness. Occasionally he would enter my room without noticing me or any one else, so that I could only know of his presence by the waving of his long cloak, as he glided from the door to the window. At other times he would come to the foot of the bed, and, without seeming conscious that I observed him, would eye me with a look in which pity for me seemed to temper the extremest depth of sullen indignation. But if I spoke to him, instantly all moroseness or vindictiveness would drop from his countenance. He would listen with affectionate solicitude, and answer with an attention the most studiously gracious. By degrees his care found a refuge at my bedside. There he would sit, smoking and talking of his anger and his sorrow ; glorying in having always defended and admired the political wisdom of Pitt ; and listening with lively interest to my opinions about the persevering assistance that Spain might expect from Great Britain.

"O Don Carlos," he would exclaim, " if, with the assistance of God and of England, we could once sweep away these pestilent devils! If once we could plant the foot of our defence in the rugged defiles of the Pyrenees! Then, while our blood streamed there, poor Spain within might draw breath, and revive from her wounds, and be again herself. O Antonio, Antonio! how often, when thou hast eulogised the pacific wisdom of Fox—when thou hast demanded why England could not, like Spain, be at peace with Bonaparte—how often have I said to thee, ' Would to God the pacific wisdom of Spain may not peaceably resign her as a province to France! Would to God she could see, like Pitt, that for her there is no health but in exertion—no safety but in war!' And now, Don Carlos! What now can Antonio say to me? What, but that he was wrong! And with tears in his eyes does he now acknowledge it !"

At length Don Manoel, calmed by such expression of his trouble, would not refuse those little consoling attentions which the women of his country render to the dignity of man. He submitted his chin to the barber, and suffered his person to be tended as usual.

CHAPTER XI

I HAVE not proceeded thus far in my narrative without many admonitions from that repugnance which all men, in the occasional remissions of vanity, must feel in giving a long history of themselves. I struggle against this diffident reluctance, not because my vainer hours persuade me it is unfounded, but from a conviction that whenever I should hereafter perceive those impressive scenes of my life to fade and mingle in the retrospect as I left them farther, and still farther, behind me, I should feel incessant regret had idleness or ill-timed diffidence withheld me from fixing them beyond the transitory power of my memory. But, as I have no pleasure in writing anything that others are not to read, it behoves me to dress it in some degree for them, and to check myself in the diffuseness of egotism, that my narrative may not outlive the interest I wish it to excite. As in this view it appeared unreasonable to have occupied so many pages in detailing the events of a fortnight,

I have glanced back upon the matter they contain, and would unsparingly have curtailed it, but that my judgment, I confess, has acquitted it of prolixity. Peculiar circumstances attend this part of my history, which perhaps exempt it from the obligation of conciseness and dispatch which can seldom be well dispensed with in private memoirs; and I hope I am not misled by that purblind affection with which we are apt to look on our own works, when I conceive the causes of its bulk to furnish its apology. It is distended by the dialogues I have introduced; but, if I estimate rightly the curiosity of my readers, it will not be uninteresting to know how extraordinary circumstances acted upon foreigners respecting whose character and opinions the spirit of inquiry in this country has met with much contradictory information. Faithfully and simply to narrate facts is to exclude the operation of prejudice; and it is giving my readers as fair an opportunity of judging as I possessed myself, if I state with truth what were the expressions of those people, when the nature of co-existent circumstances would naturally call forth the sentiments of the heart. This I have endeavoured to do. I have avoided drawing any inferences from the conversations I have related, and have written them from a careful effort of the memory—never of the invention. In translating the speeches of foreigners who spoke in their own language, I could always swear to the substance, and very often to the words.

The preceding pages are also distended by a minute attention to the effect of passing events upon my own feelings—in short, to the state of my mind during the pressure of an event which changed for ever my corporeal frame, and cannot be supposed insignificant in its influence on my future life. While health and hope, in the effervescent fervour of youth, gave something of a magic colouring to the prospects before me—while, warm in heart and joyous in mind, the present seemed capable of but little improvement—one of those chance blows that are always impending over human enjoyment had fallen and wrought a change. By dwelling upon that serious change, effected amid circumstances of exasperation and dismay, it is· discovered that still much softness and mercy were suffered to mingle in the cup of calamity, not adventitiously found, but seemingly provided as the natural and innate shelter of a guiltless[1] mind; and in weighing the natural effects of a consciousness so delightful, it may be concluded that the influence of this change upon my future life will be beneficial. If so, I must consider laudable the greatest minuteness in giving details which seem to

---

[1] The candour inspired by the tranquil gravity of my subject has betrayed me into an expression that sounds like the language of self-praise. By " guiltless mind " I mean no more than a clear conscience !

authorise inferences so productive of confidence and courage.

Let not those who are untouched imagine that I clothe with undue importance an event that has happened to so many. It is not the less important because common. Death is common also; yet who, approaching his icy hand, has contemplated his stroke as less important because aimed alike against all mankind? Though of less magnitude than the change of death, of no trifling pressure is that alteration by which, from the buoyancy of adolescence, a transition is made to the slow and painful gait of irrecoverable lameness. Dear to me, and doubly dear because snatched away, is the free bound of exuberant youth. Dear the erect port, and the easy, deliberate, even pace of graver manhood! Ever to be regretted, when lost, is the enviable power

To wander pensive through the silent groves,

or to range unfettered over the face of nature. Nor is there one movement, one sport, one exercise dependent on agility, but receives, as lost, a tenfold value in my mind.

These are regrets which follow my misfortune; nor perhaps are these the worst! But these and worse, had I no consolation but the blessings that remain, I trust I should bear withour a murmur. The mind is still itself. There is health, and with it the spirit at least and the gaiety of heart that belong to youth ; and if misfortune has deprived me of its activity, it is well to recollect that fortune enables me to move without it. The love of my friends is undiminished. It is they who have most lamented my distress. The social affections of life are mine! Nor is there any character, full of hope, to the feeling heart, that excludes me from its cheering promises. And are not these enough? Ought I to deem the misfortune too severe which has left me the possession of these? No! The blessings that remain are enough to reconcile me to the blow. But if, while it has impaired the structure of my body, it may have improved the temper of my mind, if, imbibing under its pressure a great and momentous lesson, the mind may have learned to contemplate unappalled the extremes of misfortune in the instructed confidence that we are never abandoned ; if, remembering the merciful softness with which its bitterness was tempered, I should own an enlivened gratitude to God (and even a better acquaintance with Him)—then who would wonder if not only I ceased to regret it, but, deeming it a blessing more than a misfortune, I would not even wish it to be recalled?

CHAPTER XII

AFTER so long a digression, it may be necessary to
remind the reader that my narrative has to be continued from the 11th of August, when my two
friends, de la Platière and Simon, took their leave,
having first brought to my acquaintance General
Girard's aide-de-camp. Of this gentleman I have
forgotten nothing but the name. His attentions
to me were unremitting, delicate, and unobtrusive.
Whatever·he could discover I was in want of, he
was industrious to procure; and came himself with
plentiful supplies of coffee, sugar, and wine.

On the 14th I was informed that a British
commissary who had fallen into the enemy's hands
had just arrived at Talavera on his way to the
English army, under a passport from King Joseph.
A day or two before, Mr. Higgins had delivered
to me a message from Colonel Bathurst, Sir Arthur
Wellesley's Secretary, most kindly offering his
services, either in transmitting letters or messages
to my friends or in any other way that I should
point out. Taking advantage, therefore, of the

opportunity which this commissary's arrival offered,
I wrote to Colonel Bathurst as follows:—

TALAVERA DE LA REGNA, 14th August 1809.

MY DEAR COLONEL,—I return you many thanks for
your inquiries and offer, communicated to me by Mr.
Higgins, the principal surgeon here.

My health continues very good, and my stump is
going on very well: from what the surgeon says, I hope
to be at Madrid in the course of two or three weeks.

I am sure you will be glad to give this information to
my brother,—perhaps it would be more satisfactory to
send him this letter.

Pray, if you can, advise him as to any exertions that
may tend to enable me to return to England when recovered, either on parole or by exchange.   I should hope
that, being (for the present at least) *hors de combat*, the
thing might be managed.   Pray tell General Sherbrooke,
with my best regards, that I wrote to him on the 9th,
enclosing a letter for my father, which General Séméllé
Chef de l'État, Major to the Corps commanded by Victor,
kindly promised me should reach its destination.

We are treated very kindly by the French, and it is
said that the King has interested himself about us.

Say everything kind from me to Colonel Fletcher, and
believe me, with repeated thanks, my dear Colonel, very
truly yours,   CHARLES BOOTHBY.

Lieut.-Col. Bathurst.

This letter, which Colonel Bathurst hastened to
forward, reached my family before that of the 9th,

and, being the first of my handwriting they saw
after my misfortune, gave the first touch of joy to
their sorrowing hearts.

About this time, my friend Taylor, having recovered sufficiently to move about with the help of
a stick, paid me a visit. My soup was about to
be served ; so he seated himself by the bed, and we
dined together. This unusual pleasure drew me
into too much effort of conversation, and he left
me fatigued and dejected. About the 18th he
wrote to me, complaining bitterly of the misery of
his abode. " My sleep," he said, " is broken, and
my uncertain appetite disgusted and driven away,
by the deadly smell of a hospital and the groans
of the dying. Make room for me if you can, and
rescue me from this house of despair ! " I immediately consulted the good Pollonia, who, happy
in the thought of obliging me and erecting a
barrier against the French officers, delayed not her
preparation. On the 19th, therefore, Taylor
joined me ; which, now that I began to regain my
strength, was a great amendment in my way of
life ; for he was a kind, open-hearted fellow, full
of spirit and entertainment. We joined our estab-
lishments in the utmost harmony, except that his
Englishman and my Italian used to amuse us by
their petty disputes ; the surly growling of the
one and the pert chattering of the other, in
languages as dissimilar as their manners, formed a

remarkable contrast.   One day, however, their
discordance took rather a more serious complexion.
Pedro had passed some jest upon the Englishman,
which, being delivered in Spanish, cut him off from
all hope of retort, whilst he saw the Spanish women
convulsed with laughter at his expense.   The only
answer which suggested itself to John was a
thundering box on the grinning Italian's ear.
Pedro, snatching up a large knife, with which he
had been skinning eels, and swearing vehemently
in every language he had ever heard, made John
distinctly understand that his purpose was to stick
it into him.   Shocked beyond measure at so inhuman an idea, John rushed to his master pale and
trembling, and began to utter the most grievous
complaints.

"What the devil ?" cried his master.   "Can't
you manage an Italian ?   If he runs his rigs upon
you, can't you take and thump him ?"

"I did thump him," John blubbered forth,
"and he was going to stab me with a long knife!"

John in tears!   Far from softening the heart
of his warlike master, it served only to excite an
alternation of ridicule and anger; and dismissing
him with a volley of the most contemptuous reproaches, Taylor called upon me to join his mirth,
which I could not help doing.   Yet I apprised
Pedro that if in his disputes he ever again dared
to have recourse to a knife, the first use it should

be put to would be to cut off his own ears—a threat at which he appeared less terrified than diverted.

The day after Taylor joined me, I had for the first time left my bed, and, seated in an elbow-chair, was carried to table in an outer room. This was at first a delightful change; but I was so much reduced and enfeebled that, the sitting posture soon becoming painful, in less than an hour I was glad to be laid again in the bed, and rest myself from this extraordinary fatigue.

Day by day, however, the difficulty diminished, and I was able to sit up longer, which restored to me the grateful change of occupation and rest. While I had lain in bed there was no outward sign constantly before my eyes of the loss my frame had sustained; but when, refreshed with reviving strength, I had risen from the sick-bed, the deficiency was ever before me, to carry a pang to my heart; and it was now that I had to combat some feelings of regret, not perhaps unnatural, which I afterwards condemned as unmanly and ungrateful; and they fled before the reasoning supplied by calm reflection. Meantime the progress of cure was not so favourable as had been expected. The disposition in the muscles to retract required a tightness of bandage which made me suffer extremely and broke my rest; but as I became accustomed to it I bore it better. The perseverance of Mr. Higgins in this painful remedy warded off a predicament which in other cases was the cause of prolonged suffering, danger, or death. Taylor and myself lived very pleasantly and profitably together. Our breakfast consisted of tea, dry toast, and abundance of fresh eggs. After breakfast, I was replaced upon the bed with a book ; and he used to walk out till dinner-time, and then return with all the current news, and perhaps with Higgins as our guest. Then I, having been refreshed by quiet and composure, was very sprightly for the repast, and we generally attacked it with merriment and spirit ; this more particularly when, by the arrival of a French sutler, we were enabled to heighten it with a bottle of claret. Pedro was an excellent cook, and made us eel pies and *stoffatos ;* while as a standing dish the neat-handed Catalina prepared her incomparable *ollapodrida.*

The following letter is illustrative of our way of life at this time :—

TALAVERA DE LA REGNA, 25th *August* 1809.

MY EVER DEAREST FATHER,—My limb, after a good deal of struggling, owing to a propensity in the muscles to retract, is now almost healed. I have quite recovered my appetite, and have got a friend to come and live with me, and we have very comfortable little dinners. I have great hopes that we shall get our liberty, as soon as able to undertake a long journey ; at any rate, I feel confident that if I go to King Joseph's levy on my crutches and present my petition, it will not be refused.

I assure you, I could write in the gayest spirits, if I did not know that this letter would find you all in melancholy plight.

I wrote you a letter dated the 9th, to tell you how wrong it was to repine, and to scold you for your grief when you heard I had lost my leg. I assure you, the thoughts of the happy—many happy—days I shall spend in the midst of you, have lightened my sleepless nights, and have made me feel deeply grateful to God ; not that I attribute to the Almighty any interference in the direction of the bullet, but I thank Him for so tempering the human mind as to enable it to draw consolation from itself at the very instant when the heaviest calamities assail the body.

I shall, please God, return to you fresh, healthy, gay, and happy. Do not alter this by repining yourselves at that which now cannot be remedied—but might have been so much, so very much worse. My kindest love to all. God bless thee, dearest Father !—Yours ever the same, on one leg or two,   CHARLES.

Spiral Mountain at Villafranca from which France is seen (p. 257).

CHAPTER XIII

It was but a few days longer that I had the pleasure of Taylor's society. Hoping that the comfort of his situation, if not his prospect of exchange, would be improved by going to Madrid, he joined with other officers and accompanied a convoy proceeding to that capital. Before this period some British officers had removed thither. We had at first heard that the King made them his particular care. Afterwards a rumour circulated that some severity was resorted to, in consequence of an escape; but this rumour died away, and did not deter these officers from following.

Soon after Taylor's departure, my thoughts, as I began to promise myself ability to travel, turned towards my liberation. Marshal Victor had, on his own authority, exchanged several officers, and left with others their written freedom. Mortier might have the same power; and that he would not want the inclination I trusted from the accounts which Higgins had given me of his frankness and urbanity, to which, indeed, my friend now urged me to appeal.   On the 29th of August, therefore, I wrote to Marshal Mortier (who is Duke of Treviso), stating my case and the anxiety that preyed upon my mind.   I received his answer next day.   It was as follows :—

M. Charles Boothby, Capitaine au Corps Royal du
    Génie, de l'armée Britannique, à Talavera.

Au Q. Gênal. à Oropesa, le 30 Aoust 1809.

Monsieur,—Je viens de recevoir la lettre que vous m'avez écrite hier.   J'adresse à Madrid la demande de votre échange, et je prie S.E. le Major-Général d'avoir égard à la position où vous vous trouvez.   Je m'empresserai de vous faire connaître sa réponse.   En attendant, Monsieur, disposez de moi, ainsi que vos camarades, si je puis vous être utile à quelque chose.—J'ai l'honneur de vous saluer,   Le Mal. Duc de Trevise.

Translation

Headquarters, Oropesa, 30th August 1809.

Sir,—I have just received the letter which you wrote to me yesterday.   I address to Madrid the demand of your exchange, and I beg His Excellency the Major-General to have regard to your particular situation.   I shall hasten to let you know his answer.   In the meantime, sir, make use of me—your comrades likewise—if I can be at all useful to you.—I have the honour to salute you,

The Marshal Duke of Treviso.

As I had indulged the hope that Mortier himself would have the power to let me go, his letter, kind as it was, disappointed me ; yet I still hoped for a favourable answer from Jourdan, to whom he had referred my petition.

I think it was before this time that Colonel Donelan of the 48th Regiment died.

My own memoir promises to be so long that I do not profess to record in it the events which happened to my fellow-prisoners, however worthy of narration ; but I should not be satisfied to omit the name of Colonel Donelan, who displayed yet more heroism in contemplating the sure approach of his last hour than when, glowing with glorious courage, and cheering his men in the thickest of the battle, he received the fatal wound. The French showed to his remains the greatest respect, and their superior officers joined our own in following them to the grave, wherein he was laid with military honours.

Early in September I had the pleasure to receive letters from the army—from Mulcaster, Colonel Bathurst, and General Sherbrooke. I copy the two last.—

From Colonel Bathurst

22nd August 1809.

MY DEAR SIR,—I have sent home your letter to your brother, which, I hope, will give him pleasure, as it appeared to be written in good spirits. General Sher-

brooke also wrote to your father by the same opportunity.

Sir Arthur has written to Mortier to request that such
officers as are able to move may be allowed to return on
their parole.   I advise you to apply for this yourself to
the French Commander-in-Chief, or direct to King
Joseph, stating your situation; and I think you will
succeed.

I have got a small quantity of tea, which I send to
such as I know at Talavera; I am sorry it is not more—
I have only two pounds.   I wish you would divide one
with Stanhope of the 29th, and the other between Major
Popham, 24th, and Milman of the Guards.   If I have any
opportunity, I will try to send more.—Believe me, ever
sincerely yours,   JAMES BATHURST.

Captain Boothby.

From General Sherbrooke

24th August 1809.

MY DEAR BOOTHBY,—On the return of Mr. Commissary Dillon from Talavera, I immediately wrote to
your father to inform him of the very favourable accounts
which I had received of you, and of the very handsome
manner in which, I understood, the whole of our prisoners
had been treated by the French.

I hope that, when you acquire sufficient strength to
be moved, Marshal Victor will allow you to come away
upon parole; and should there be any French officer of
your rank (about whom he may interest himself) a
prisoner in England, I will use my utmost endeavours to
have him sent back, in exchange for you.

I beg you will let me hear from you by every
opportunity, as I not only am anxious to learn how you

are coming on, but am particularly desirous to send information on so interesting a subject to your father and mother.

With every wish for the speedy and perfect re-establishment of your health, believe me, my dear Boothby, yours with great esteem and regard,   J. C. SHERBROOKE.

The kindness of these letters and of that from Mulcaster naturally gave me much pleasure. What they recommended, however, as a means of procuring my liberty, I had already done ; and it was needless to communicate to Mortier General Sherbrooke's offer, since I had found that the discretion necessary to act on it did not rest in him.

The bed in which I slept was in a sort of recess, which might be separated from the rest of the room by drawing a curtain. On getting up, I had used to be carried to a window in the outer room, which, having a northern aspect, was cool and refreshing ; but, though from this situation I could hear all that passed in the street, I could see nothing of it. About the 10th of September, I complained of this to Catalina, who instantly suggested that, if I would have myself carried into the passage and sit there, I should see all down the street. Accordingly, I was carried into the passage, and instantly found myself once more in the world. The change which this trifling move wrought on my thoughts and feelings was incredible. I eyed everything with rapture; but chiefly a luxuriant fig-tree in full leaf, which, growing in the midst of the yard, thrust its broad fresh leaves over the balcony. Since my eyes had had nothing to dwell on but dirty white walls and the wretched images of Saints which hung thereon, they had become sadly weary. For more than six weeks I had seen no tree or growing thing; and I cannot express the delight with which I dwelt on every part of this fig-tree, curiously examining its manner of growth, from the substantial trunk through each twist of the branches to the consummate leaves:

> First from the root springs lighter the green stalk,
> And then the leaves more airy—last the bright
> Consummate flower spirit odorous breathes!

I had never considered a fig-tree very wonderful before; but now it did indeed almost seem a miraculous thing.

On my right hand was a window, down to the ground, with a wooden balcony. Through this I surveyed the yard where the tree grew; where, also, the multiplied business of house and stable was by various hands proceeding. It seemed that I compared all that I now saw, not with like things which my eye had before been familiar with, but only with the pictures of such things. It seemed, in short, as if I were now viewing the reality of

things, which I had hitherto seen only in picture!
This was, I suppose, from my looking at everything
with such avidity that no lineament of it escaped
me, as we naturally do look at good pictures of
common objects. For example, a man grooming
a horse had not before seemed worthy of close
observation; but any good drawing of it I had in-
stinctively examined minutely.   Now, long confinement caused me to examine the reality with equal
minuteness; and, consequently, the mind compared
what it now contemplated with the picture on
which it had bestowed the like attention, not with
the reality, which it had always viewed in a cursory
manner.

In front of my chair was the staircase, by which
all visitors were subject first to my inspection; and
over the stairs was a window, through which the
whole length of the great street was laid open to
my view.   It is worthy of remark, how much may
often be done for comfort by little trouble.   Just
carrying my chair three yards farther had obtained
for me a constant variety of interest and amuse-
ment; for now I could interrupt my reading by
occasionally hearing the remarks of the women as
they performed the business of the house.   This
would often draw us into conversation; thence
came laughter, or gossiping anecdote; and time flew!

One morning, soon after this discovery, on
my calling for Pedro, I found that he was gone

out. As he did not come soon, I sent for Aaron, who, with a sleepy face, said that he believed Pedro had run away !

" Why do you think so ? " said I, feeling sure that it was so.

" Because he has taken his things : I saw him packing them up last night."

The women now began to exclaim, and, coming to me, begged that I should instantly ascertain if he had robbed me.

" Far from it ! " said I. " Yesterday he asked me for only half the wages due to him, which I gave him,—so that I am still in his debt."

They expressed great satisfaction at these tidings ; and we presently acquitted little Pedro of all blame, and wished him a safe and prosperous journey.

He had stayed by me faithfully until I was becoming well, and able to do with little assistance, and then he had taken the liberty to think a little of himself. He might as easily have had from me the whole as the half of his wages. Perhaps this forbearance sprang from the fear of exciting my suspicion ; but if from that of leaving me ill-provided, how very amiable was his moderation ! Somebody met him on the day of his flight, near Naval Moral, by whom he sent his duty to me; and I have never heard of him since.

I had passed the expected time of my cure,

which was retarded by unforeseen circumstances, prolonging my suffering and uncertainty.   My strength, however, had rallied so effectually as to withstand the local relapse ; and the progress of my health continued.

On the 14th of September I wrote letters to the army, enclosing one for my father to General Sherbrooke.   These I sent to Mortier, with a request that he would forward them.   I knew not yet how my family had borne the news of my disaster; and, judging from the fervent love I had ever experienced from them, I dreaded that their affliction would be unbounded.   My chief anxiety, therefore, was to convince them that I myself was content, and to send them such pictures of my present state as to do away any despairing ones their sorrow might have painted.   Such was the object of the following letter :—

TALAVERA DE LA REGNA, 14th September 1809.

MY EVER DEAREST FATHER,—I enclose this to General Sherbrooke, and entreat the Duke of Treviso (Mal. Mortier) to forward it to him, which, unless there be any real difficulty, I am persuaded he will do ; so that I have good hopes this letter will reach you.   I have already told you that you are not to repine at the loss of my leg. I shall bounce upon you some day, expecting to find happiness and compensation among you.   Think how I shall be disappointed to find you have all worn yourselves away in useless, pernicious pining !

In justice to me, and that you may be able to afford me
the resources I shall seek, do not grieve for a loss that
cannot be recalled.   I dwell more on this subject than I
should, from an expression which I remember my mother
used when John Lumley lay ill.   She thought, *to have a
leg cut off was little better than dying.*   I remember the
observations of Philip Pierrepont equally well; they are
more consoling : " He can ride, he can drive, he can walk,
and at six o'clock he's as good a man as any ! "

Look to the bright side, dearest Father, and be you as
easy on the subject as I am, and it will soon be forgotten.

My cure has been retarded by an unexpected retro-
grade, but now it will probably be completed in a day
or two.

I was very fortunately lodged in the house of a kind,
good old woman, who was very much affected at my
misfortune.   Poor soul ! she begged and entreated they
would not take off the leg (for, owing to their want of
skill, I believe they consider it a very hazardous operation).   She came to me and proposed that some Saint or
other should touch it, but I told her I wanted faith !

Now that I am up all day, and grown convivial, and
make a deal of noise in the house, the old lady and I joke
one another all day long !   There is another dark, lively,
dancing woman in the house who is entirely under my
orders ; and while she sits at work, I try to impede it by
making her laugh.

The surgeon has forbade my mounting the crutches
hitherto, but I sit in a situation whence I enfilade the
principal street and see all that passes.

My companion is gone to Madrid, but I generally
have somebody to dine with me, and am already no bad
table companion !

I intended to cast over this letter a sort of decorous formality, as I must send it open ; but I have been drawn out as it were, and there does not seem much restraint. The weather is less hot, which is a great delight.

My only restlessness is about you all ; follow my advice, and this will not be such a blow as perhaps it has appeared to you. Give my kindest love ! God for ever bless you, dearest Father !—Ever your most affectionate and dutiful son, CHARLES.

Peasants winding Flax.

CHAPTER XIV

THOUGH I have said much of the Spanish women, perhaps I have not made the reader acquainted with all the inhabitants of the house, every one of whom, in a greater or less degree, contributed to my comfort and entered into my acquaintance. By us, who keep such an impassable line between our own society and that of our servants, it cannot easily be conceived how freely, in the middle ranks of Spain, the two classes associate with each other. All the individuals under the same roof are treated as beings of equal natures. They have, indeed, different duties to perform—some to direct, others to obey—yet they are equally entitled to observance and consideration. Thus all contribute, according to their social talents, to furnish the family circle. Strange to say, this system, which should seem calculated to disturb the due subordination, appears to have an effect directly opposite. The submissive docility of the servants keeps pace with the urbanity and affability with which their masters treat them.

After these observations, the nature and variety of my domestic circle at Talavera will be the more easily understood. Don Manoel and Doña Pollonia have been already introduced to the reader ; but these good people were not really entitled to such noble distinctions. Wherever I have been on the Continent of Europe, there has seemed to be a very lavish commerce with the titles of nobility. In Naples and Sicily every stranger not raggedly dressed was by the needy and expectant natives styled " Your Excellency" or " Your Lordship" ; and every house, above a cottage, was by courtesy termed the Palace. I had a Sicilian groom who invariably used to say to me, " At what hour shall I bring Your Excellency's horse to the palace ?" So in Spain and Portugal the title of " Your Grace" is generally and indiscriminately used, and even passes between beggars. It was, I suppose, from this habit of bestowing liberally what may be so easily given that the inmates of the house called its mistress and her sons Don and Doña; and I naturally adopted it from them. Besides, they called me Don Carlos !

Don Antonio (a Don of the same description) was a lodger in the house, and much respected—a quiet, sensible, agreeable man. Next in consequence came Catalina—a tall, elegant woman of forty, whose dark complexion and jetty eyes gave great expression to agreeable features. She was more like a housekeeper than a common servant, and was held in the highest estimation by the Señora, who had known her from a child, and could not relish the *olla*, she told me, unless Catalina had put her hand to it.   The inferior servants consisted of two old women, employed as charwomen, and a country wench as a house-lass. The old women were called Tia Maria and Tia Pepa ; for, though the word *tia* means only aunt, it is commonly applied to such old women, even though their brothers and sisters should be childless.   The name of the girl was Manoela—a lively, very simple, hard-working lass—plain, hale, and hardy, and capable of chastising with her fists any ill-mannered youth who gave her the least impertinence.

Each of the ladies allowed me to take a sketch of her person ; and it was generally acknowledged (apart from the opinion of the subject) that each portrait was pretty successful.

But these were not all, nor yet the most agreeable, of my Spanish company.   Soon after my feast of the fig-tree, which occasioned me to see so much more of what passed in the house, I was much struck with the appearance of a beautiful little creature playing in the yard.   This, they told me, was la Marta, one of the daughters of Augustin, the carpenter.   I soon became acquainted with this little beauty, and not long after with her sister, who had just grown into all the elegance and slender grace of a finely-formed damsel. Her face was not so beautiful, not so sparkling, as that of Martita ; but it was more lovely, more replete with feminine charm. Maria Dolores was in temper different from her little sister. She was pensive, tender, and, though not reluctant to laugh, did not herself move to mirth. That boneless simplicity of dress so advantageous to the female figure, when nature does not need constraint, gave its full lustre to the beauty of the young Maria. I remember the pliant stays, close grasping her thin waist, from the end of which a dark petticoat fell, not low enough to conceal how finely her legs and feet were made, nor how neatly they were clothed. Linen sleeves rolled up above her elbows exhibited smooth arms of alabaster. A handkerchief, gathered about her throat in white but impervious folds, gave in modesty more beauty than it concealed. Her face, of an expression the most intellectual and a colouring the most pure and evanescent, blushed beneath the shade of her luxuriant hair, of a dark yet burnished brown, floating in broad artless curls from where it was attempted to restrain them. Such really was Maria Dolores. I am sensible that the description does not seem to suit a carpenter's daughter; but those who beheld her thought only of beauty in its sweetest prime and softest gentleness, "when unadorned, adorned the most."

These fair sisters, interested in my misfortune, and pleased with the kindness and openness of my manner, used to play about me with the familiarity and gentleness of kittens, and lightened many an hour. I was indebted for much of the society of Maria to those charms which made it so agreeable; for a French officer who lodged in the house of Augustin fell desperately in love with her and, because the parents wisely sent her to their neighbour's house, to keep her out of his way, used to be transported with fury.

The motions of the different corps, however, after a time took away this ungovernable lover and brought back my friend de la Platière. On the 19th of September, before I had done dressing, he brushed up with his wonted haste, and, suddenly embracing me, kissed each side of my face. Though somewhat disconcerted by this unusual mode of salutation, I was extremely glad to see him. He told me that Villatte's corps would enter the town in the course of the day, Marshal Mortier being destined to pursue the Spanish army.

He soon left me to finish my toilette.

When, having breakfasted, I had assumed my post in the passage, a French officer came to me, saying that General Séméllé had sent him to inquire how I did, and if I stood in need of his good offices. I was sitting in conversation with this officer when de la Platière returned, bringing

me a letter from Mortier, of which the following
is a copy :—

OROPESA, *le* 19 *Septembre* 1809.

MONSIEUR,—Son Excellence M. le Maréchal Jourdan,
à qui je vous ai marqué que j'avois écrit relativement à
la demande que vous faites de votre échange, vient de me
répondre que S.M.C. lui avoit donné l'ordre de la sou-
mettre au Ministre de la guerre à Paris.

Je désire, Monsieur, que la décision du Ministre réponds
à votre attente, et que cette démarche ait tout le succès
que vous pouvez souhaiter.

Je profiterai de l'occasion du premier Parlementaire
pour envoyer au Général de l'armée Anglaise les lettres
que vous m'adressez pour M. votre père.—J'ai l'honneur,
Monsieur, de vous saluer,

LE MAL. DUC DE TREVISE.

Translation

OROPESA, 19*th September* 1809.

SIR,—His Excellency the Marshal Jourdan, to whom,
as I have informed you, I had written relative to the
demand you make for your exchange, now answers me
that His Catholic Majesty had given him orders to submit
it to the Minister of War at Paris.

I wish, sir, that the decision of the Minister may
answer your expectation, and that this proceeding may
have all the success you yourself can wish.

I will avail myself of the opportunity of the first flag
of truce in order to send to the General of the English
army the letters which you send to me for your father.
—I have the honour, sir, to salute you.

THE MARSHAL DUKE OF TREVISO.

8

I concealed, beneath as gay an air as I could summon, the. bitter disappointment which the perusal of this letter caused ; but de la Platière, having read it, seemed rather disposed to congratulate me upon its contents.

After General Sémélé's aide - de - camp had departed, however, and I had been carried into my room, he said, " I perceive that the Marshal's letter vexes you. You are wrong to let it. I can tell you exactly how all that will be managed. When you are well, you will go to Madrid. Refresh yourself there! See all that it contains! It is not Paris ; but it does not want resource. You will be very well amused for a time. When you are tired, purchase a commodious carriage and travel quietly to France! Spend three delightful months in Paris (you cannot see it in less than that), and then you will be exchanged."

He said all this in such a flourishing manner that I was in doubt whether to be comforted or provoked,— a balance which enabled my good-humour to come forward, and I consented to be amused. But I would not acquiesce in the plan he had laid down as long as a hope remained that I should be allowed to go to Lisbon instead of to Madrid. General Sémélé, I remembered, said, when I first saw him, that he himself could exchange me but for my inability to travel. I was now able to travel. Did he still retain the power to release me? I thought it worth asking, and wrote to him for that purpose.

I was at dinner, enlivened by de la Platière's conversation, when, to answer my letter, and to satisfy his own good feelings, General Séméllé called upon me.

" Ne vous dérangez pas," he said, as he entered ; and, quickly sitting down, added that it would give him great pleasure to see me finish my repast with a good appetite. Then, adverting to the letter I had just written to him, he informed me that he had forwarded to Madrid a list of such British officers as were mutilated, with such a strong recommendation as he hoped would effect their speedy release. He spoke of the battle, eulogised the English troops, and observed of Sir Arthur Wellesley, " Assurément c'est un homme de talent—oui ! il a démontré un grand génie pour la guerre—il a beaucoup de talent !—beaucoup ! il n'y a rien de plus sûr ! " General Séméllé, had he commanded the French troops, would have attacked the Spaniards mainly, while he made a brisk reconnaissance upon our part of the line. Before he went away, he good-humouredly laid his commands on de la Platière to befriend me with zeal, and entreated me upon all occasions to command his own services without reserve.

This interview but little increased my prospect of liberty, and I began to think it so remote and uncertain that I indulged less in dreams of return. I was now almost constantly in the society of de la Platière, who, deeming solitude the most pitiable of evils, and especially, as he said, *quand on dine*, came to me invariably at dinner, in order (as he expressed himself) to make his court to me. But, unfortunately, either from a national or from an individual peculiarity, it is in some degree irksome to me to dine in the presence of a friend who is not dining. Therefore I used to say to him, "Eat—I must insist upon you eating; for I cannot without horror sit devouring here while you do nothing." It was to no purpose. Neither would he eat nor suffer me to dine alone. As now my health was more assured, and we knew one another better, we disputed freely. With an unusual degree of national vanity, even for a Frenchman, he possessed an immovable good-nature which ensured an amiable close to our debates. Among other things equally provoking, he said that if a single ship of France and another of England, each of equal force in all respects, were to come to close quarters at sea, there was no doubt that the French ship would gain the victory. Our Admirals were better, he said; therefore our fleets prevailed; but, ship to ship, the French must beat, because they would rather sink than strike.

"And I believe," said I, "that wherever the experiment has been tried your ship has been

obliged to do one or the other. These sentiments, my friend, are natural for you to en-
courage. I entertain those which I hope equally
become me; but I should never have insisted
on them in conversation with a Frenchman. I
have never yet told you that I think our soldiers
superior to yours; yet I feel as sure of it as
that our fleets are so."

"Non! non! non! non! non! Mon cher
Capitaine!—ah! bah! bah!—par terre, vous ne
pouvez plus lutter contre nous! non! non! par
terre, notre supériorité est parfaitement décidé.
C'est une chose qu'actuellement on ne peut plus
disputer!"

"By numbers you are superior—that indeed,
cannot be disputed. You outnumber us so that
we can but seldom look you in the face. When
we do, I do not think we have your other
superiority so very evident. Mon cher ami, you
know I can bring an example, respecting which
we can neither of us be misinformed. How have
your 45,000 men been received here by 20,000
British?"

"You count for nothing, then," said he,
" 50,000 Spaniards?"

"Their amount, on paper, before the battle was
30,000. And recollect that it was only the other
day that you yourself branded these Spaniards
with ignominy for not firing a shot."

Facts were here so much against him that he could only account for them by the extraordinary skill of General Wellesley and the blunders of Victor—ending by a remark (with which perhaps he had better have begun) that on national subjects it was not to be expected we should come to an accordance of opinion.

But we agreed no better on points still more important. He said that he would rather die than suffer all I must have gone through. I answered that I must appear to him a much more forlorn and miserable object than I was disposed to think myself.

"Ah, non!" said he. "You have got through it; but I speak of when you received your wound, and, after a great deal of cutting and torturing proposed, life was to be very uncertain. That protracted suffering and being coolly carved with a great knife is intolerable. No: I had rather die. On est tué—c'est fini! On meurt sur la champ de bataille—c'est en règle!—on y meurt avec gloire! but to linger, and in cold blood to have one's best limbs severed from one in the flower of one's age! Ah! Dieu! C'est terrible! Non, mon cher! In such a case I have always a little store of opium to secure me from protracted torments!"

"How," said I, "do you know that opium would end them?"

"I would take enough to kill me!"

"You would die ; but are you sure that dying would accomplish the view with which you would commit suicide ? "

"Ah, mon cher ! si vous allez parler de l'autre monde, it is what we can neither of us know any-thing about. No, no ! I regard death as the end. If I am to live again, 'tis not my fault. I shall make the best of it ! "

I am reluctant always to put forth to the storms of controversy opinions bereft of which I should seem such a bubble as de la Platière believed himself ; and from a Frenchman I had an especial horror of drawing upon myself a tirade of modern philosophy, which truth's clearest voice would seek in vain to silence ; for it is in the hope of drowning that clear voice that modern philosophy clamours. ·The sceptic, with all possible coolness, sits trifling with the Christian, who, on his side, shakes under the weight of the cause he defends. On the issue of the argument seems to depend the question whether he be an insect,

Born but to breathe, to suffer, and to end,

or an angel, for a while debased by a cumbrous, offensive body, but immortal, and capable, if he will, of becoming all, in grandeur, power, and knowledge, that his mind in her noblest flights has ever meditated. Anxious, alarmed, outraged, he is easily provoked by metaphysical substitutes which he wants the patience to examine ; and the dispute ends, leaving him who has been arguing for more than life worsted and wounded ; while he who has had nothing at stake but his ingenuity withdraws in triumph.

Yet with great reluctance I left de la Platière sunk where I found him !

" If," said I, " your own mind does not tell you there is another life, argument is vain."

" Il peut être," answered he,—" il peut être que j'ai mes rêves de l'immortalité, aussi bien qu'un autre ! "

When reason, enchanted with her powers, gives herself up to her own conceit, and will not only go alone, but predetermines to leave the beaten path, what a fool she makes of herself! God and the Devil—without which the making of man, and man's too evident depravity, are un-accountable—she stupidly stigmatises as extravagant fables ; and the noble aims of the misguided soul, instead of being gleams really divine, are only " des rêves de l'immortalité ! "

Such is the steadiness of her incredulity against the clearest evidence, traditional and internal, when reason sets herself to make a belief after her own fashion, immeasurable are the absurdities she swallows !

CHAPTER XV

Some of the evenings which I passed in the society I have described were diversified by the *fandango*, in which both old women and girls, coming into my room, would join for the purpose of entertaining me. The graceful figure and the tender countenance of Dolores, her long flowing hair, free and disordered by the exercise, gave a lustre to this rustic pastime ; while the beautiful Martita, acting the mischievous monkey, with an ivory grin and sparkling eyes, could do or say nothing that misbecame her. Contrasted with these were the stiff Tias, who, with stern visage and vehement gestures, seemed determined to show me that their youth had far surpassed the specimens I now beheld. Nay : so anxious were they that I should not be deceived in this particular, that the Señora herself solemnly assured me that her waist when a girl was not half so thick as that of the slender Dolores. De la Platière sometimes sat with me to survey the dance, and the kind Spaniards, won by his attention to me, had lost the connection between his presence and their horror of all his nation. Mr. Higgins had stipulated with me that I should not attempt to walk until my wound had been three days healed; Augustin had made me a pair of crutches long ago; and, my surgeon's permission being at length obtained, on the 1st of October I prepared once more to go out of that house into which, nine weeks before, I had been carried with but little hope of life. Many were the feelings which thronged within me as, tottering and slow, I crawled along over the dirty, parched pavement! The sense of attracting general observation hurried me, and made more difficult a means of walking of which I had yet had no experience. Neither the French soldiers nor the Spaniards refrained from observation as I passed. The former invariably expressed surprise at seeing the success of an amputation which in the hands of their field surgeons they knew to be almost always fatal. The Spaniards regarded me with the fondest compassion and the loudest sorrow, their affectionate sympathy touching their remarks with a colour of generous encomium.

"What a pity!" "Good God, what a pity!" "So young, too!" "Poor Englishman!" were pathetically passed along the street, and from one door to another.

Notwithstanding the difficulty with which I moved, I found such a pleasure in the glimpse of liberty that I managed to get as far as the square, where levies of officers were assembled, conversing. While resting in the shop of a traiteur, I had some conversation with Captain Christie of the Guards, who had been fortunate enough to get his exchange pre-arranged by Marshal Victor, and, being now able to travel, was to leave Talavera in a few days, for the British army. How I envied him! I returned fatigued with my walk; but it gave a value to repose and a zest to appetite which amply compensated for the labour.

I had met with General Séméllé in my walk, and the next day waited upon him to thank him for his kindness. That no time might be lost in preparation, if I should obtain my release, I put myself in treaty with a Spaniard who had just come from Madrid with a phaeton, in which he professed his readiness to take me to Lisbon; and, in order to ascertain how I could bear the motion of such a vehicle, at my request he brought it one evening to the door, drawn by two clever nags. I got up without much difficulty, and desired him to drive towards the field of battle.

Away we went at a great rate: it seemed to me now strange and enchanted, rapidly to cleave the fresh air streaming from the wild hills! The melancholy uniformity of a Spanish dwelling, the more melancholy dirt and disorder of a sacked town, had jaded my sight, which now flew with

rapture to regain the scenes of nature that it loved
—while all the events connected with those scenes
passed over the mind in a wide current of thought.
We could not get sufficiently upon the field to
satisfy my curiosity. Fragments of red and blue
dress peeping through the mounds of earth—and
here and there a human form that had escaped the
care of the buriers—brought back all that had
passed. But my wish was to gain the hill where
the British fought; there the mightiness of the
carnage had repelled all thought of burial. This,
my driver assured me, was impracticable; and I
returned much refreshed, and well pleased to have
found but little inconvenience from the motion of
the carriage, from which the fair and gentle Maria
helped me to descend, softly reproaching me for
such indications of departure.

About the 4th of October, de la Platière finally
took leave of me—Victor going from Talavera,
and the headquarters of Mortier being established
there in his room. I called upon this officer, the
Marshal Duke of Treviso, the day after his arrival.
He occupied the house which General Sémélle had
left; it had also been the quarter of General
Sherbrooke, who intended it for mine. The Duke,
not having been at home when I waited on him in
the morning, sent to beg I should dine with him.
On presenting myself at his dinner-hour, I had to
remain some time with his officers and French

guests and Sir William Sheridan (who was now
senior in rank of all the British prisoners remaining in Talavera, and was to go to Madrid the next
day). The discourse turned upon some successes
obtained by the Marshal over the rear of the
retreating Spaniards; the French officers claimed
to have taken all the Spanish artillery. The
Marshal soon entered from his private room. By
his dress and figure he might have belonged to
Frederick the Great—tall, thin, and upright, with
good features, and a countenance so clearly marked
with mild and simple honesty, combined with a
look of direct intelligence and good sense, that
whoever amid oppression had seen his head rising
above the crowd, had confidently exclaimed, "O!
that man will never suffer it! That man will
surely help us." Towards me particularly he
adopted a protecting manner at once the kindest
and the least burdensome, being so easy as to
make it seem a matter of course, and to keep the
favour of it quite out of sight. For the good
taste of such conduct did not appear to be the
result of election, but the dictate of nature. At
dinner the Spaniards were much abused, the Duke
affecting not to pique himself on the mischief he
had done them. Turning to me with a smile, he
said, " We found them taking their siesta and were
uncivil enough to wake them! They are like
sheep—to beat them is to do nothing!" A

farouche Chef d'Escadron at the other side of the table then applied to them every term of vile reproach which could be collected on so sudden an occasion.   This induced me to state my opinion that the Spaniards individually were brave, as might be shown from many instances; but any military man, I said, would have no difficulty in understanding how an army might be coward collectively though composed of very brave individuals—under bad officers and a bad organisation. The Chef d'Escadron cocked his hat, and seemed about to fire, when the Duke exclaimed that my observation was perfectly just, and that bravery might certainly be unavailing where the usage of war was wanting.   A shrug and a horrible grimace from the Chef d'Escadron notified his constrained acquiescence, and General Girard, Mortier's second in command, rallied him upon his furious hostility.

After dinner we went into another room to coffee, where the Duke held a levee, and, while conversing with his officers as to the site of our battle, turned suddenly to me.

" Do you think," said he,—" do you in your own mind believe that General Wellesley would have manœuvred in the same manner if our Emperor had been before him instead of the King of Spain ? "

Half laughing, I stated my conviction that, if the Emperor's presence would have operated at all upon Sir Arthur, it would have been in the way of attraction.

"Then," said the Duke emphatically, "without at all meaning to boast, I give you my word of honour, I have not the smallest doubt that, with the exact information which our Emperor always has, and the measures which he would most surely have taken, not one man of your army could have escaped!"

Seeing me take snuff from the box of a French officer, he asked if I liked snuff, and, finding I did not like that to be met with in Spain, "I," said he, "have some excellent French snuff"—and, sending for his valet de chambre, he ordered him to give me all he had, saying he could easily get more.

He spoke very good English when I addressed him in that language ; but he generally spoke to me in French, and asked me why I wrote to him in English since I knew French.

"I write French very ill, sir," I said, "and I knew that your Excellency spoke English like an Englishman."

He seemed much pleased to have his skill in our language thus considered, but disclaimed the compliment, saying, "I could have spoken it tolerably—I resided in England a good while when I was very young. I went there only to spend money for my father!"

On returning home, highly pleased with the

good Marshal, I was met at my room door by Don Manoel, who was in great glee at the information, which had already reached him, that the Marshal Duke had treated me with much distinction at dinner.

By degrees I became more accustomed to my crutches, was less disconcerted by the remarks that were made on me, and felt independent; for after Don Manoel had told me of all that belonged to the place, and had shown me the shortest way to the river-side, I used to go there alone, and, seated on the bank, watch that current so swiftly flowing to Lisbon, carrying with it whatever fragments of timber or other floating substances accident had committed to its course. "Those," methought, "will go without hindrance to Lisbon. Why is man's body so cumbersome, so unaccommodating? What an easy method of journeying —to lay myself upon these waves, and let myself be floated along!" About this time many of our men who had recovered found it no difficult matter to escape. I heard Mr. Higgins pressed upon this subject. He was perfectly master of his time and motions, not from having given any parole, but because those duties he so manfully undertook, which were hardly more beneficial to us than to the French, required that he should be unconfined. He was offered disguise and safe-conduct, and his success appeared to us both to be certain. The proposal was the more tempting because all the British surgeons, whose liberty one of the French Commanders had guaranteed, were now declared prisoners as well as those for whose welfare they had suffered themselves to be taken.   Neither was Mr. Higgins ignorant that, all exchange of prisoners being impracticable, the liberty and prosperity of the best years of his life would probably be sacrificed.   He felt, also, that every important part of his duty had been well performed.   Almost all the soldiers had been removed to Madrid ; his energy, his management, his mediation, were no longer wanted; and no one would now have suffered by his absence.   But he rigidly considered that while one man remained sick at Talavera of those who had been committed to his charge, duty prescribed his stay ; and all temptations to go were unavailing.

Since I had been able to go out of doors, I had become intimate with Charles Stanhope, a young officer of the 29th Regiment, who had been desperately wounded, and subsequently reduced to a shadow by illness.   It was a great resource to me to meet with one so gentlemanlike and agreeable, and he, having long been debarred from any society he liked, seemed to forward our acquaintance with no less pleasure.   He now, as well as Mr. Higgins, was often my companion at dinner, and occasionally there were one or two others.   Don Manoel enjoyed these parties.   As

9

Englishmen, he loved us all; and, with an expression of the darkest mystery, he would fasten the door as he entered, then look out of the window and all round the room, and when sure that all within hearing were honest and friendly, he used to talk in whispers of wonderful news of dangers past and hopes to come. One evening, when his heart was thus opened, the wine found an easy passage down his throat. His hat was removed, his cloak thrown back, and his dark visage was illumined by a smile but ill suited to his ghastly physiognomy. His mother came in and reproached him for his intemperance; but he had already drunk too much to be awed, even by the voice he was accustomed to honour. In the midst of her loud remonstrance, he regarded her with a satyr's grin, and filling a tumbler to the brim, swallowed it at a gulp; and immediately resuming the same grin, he gazed upon her again, till she was nearly beside herself with anger and apprehension.

"Bestia! Lojo!" she exclaimed; and then to me—"Por l' amor de Dios!—Don Carlos!"

"What can I do, señora? Can I refuse him the wine?"

Poor Manoel, however, unused to such excess, was soon glad to get out of the room, and did penance all next day.

CHAPTER XVI

HAVING been so well pleased with the Duke of Treviso's first reception of me, I was not reluctant to comply with the following invitation:—

AU QUARTIER GÉNÉRAL À TALAVERA,
Le 9 Octobre 1809.

Le Maréchal de l'Empire Mortier prie Monsieur le Capne. Boothby, de lui faire l'honneur de venir dîner chez lui aujourd'hui, à 5 heures.

Réponse s'il vous plaît.

I took this opportunity of mentioning the subject upon which I had formerly addressed him by letter, desiring his opinion as to what would probably be the answer of the Minister of War, to whom my application had been referred.

"Si vous voudrez suivre mon conseil, M. Boothby," said the Duke, "ce serait d'aller à France tout de suite! Une fois en France, il n'y a pour vous plus de difficulté! Ou si, *là*, on vous détint pour quelque temps, au moins—ce serait *en France!* Si vous vous trouvez près de l'Empereur, M. Boothby, demandez le voir!

Je suis sûr que si Sa Majesté vous voyait, Elle vous renverrait chez vous. Je vous en reponds! Si j'étais à votre place, moi, je ne perdrais pas un moment de me rendre à Madrid. Là—vous pouvez faire très commodément vos préparations de voyage. Ici—on ne trouve rien—absolument rien! Madrid est une ville de ressource! Je vais y expédier un Convoi le 14—vous conviendrat'il de vous en profiter aussitôt ?"

Very far from pleased, I could not but be convinced that, whatever difficulty there might be in the way of my release, it could not be removed in Spain ; and, accordingly, I did not hesitate (adopting the Duke's friendly advice) to turn my face towards the Pyrenees.

I said I should be glad to go to Madrid with the Convoy his Excellency had mentioned.

"But do not," said he, "let me send you away. Stay here, I beg of you, as long as you please!"

"I am aware, my Lord," I answered, "of your indulgence ; but since I am to resign the hope of going to Lisbon, I consider Madrid as a stage on my way to Paris, and the sooner it is performed the better!"

"How will you go to Madrid, Mr. Boothby?" said the Duke. "I am sorry to say I have nothing but a waggon at my disposal : you must not go in that!"

I said I was in treaty for a conveyance which I

had tried and found sufficiently commodious; at which he expressed his satisfaction.

The talk of my departure, particularly towards Madrid, gave the greatest disturbance to Maria Dolores and to the little Martita. They entreated my further stay, holding out as an inducement the hope there was that the English would return; and on the other hand, as a threat, the perpetual separation from my friends and country which would surely result, as they imagined, from my suffering myself to be taken to France. "Once in France," they said, "you are a captive for ever." I was touched with their affectionate sorrow. Doña Pollonia, with a little air of festive allurement, painted to me the social comforts of their winter hearth. If I would pass the fireside season with them, "who knows but in that time," said she, "we may see better times? Staying here, you can't be worse; but going to that infernal France, and travelling such an endless distance by land, in such a plight as yours—Jesus! Maria! what will become of you, poor thing? Aye," said she (seeing me laugh), "aye! aye!—whatever I say, always laughing! When you lay as white as a sheet and almost in the agonies of death, and I wanted the Holy Saint to be brought to touch your mangled leg—even then" (turning to the rest)—"even then—the poor thing laughed. Well, thank God for all things! It's well you've the spirit to laugh. Poor Englishman! your heart has brought you through much. The Commissary's wife said to me—the last word as she left the house—'Your poor young Englishman will die!' 'No! señora,' said I: 'it does not seem to me that he will die—tien mucho coraçon!' Si, señor!—esto dicheva Io!'" So the good old soul ran on, while the others chimed in, hoping to induce my stay.

On the 13th, in the morning, I received a kind note from the Duke of Treviso, accompanying sixteen letters, which he had taken the trouble to select from a great number sent to his outposts by Sir Arthur Wellesley. I did not know whether those from my friends in England would have left them since their knowledge of my misfortune. The blood forsook my cheek—my forehead was cold and my heart laboured within me; but on opening a letter from my father, and seeing a picture of the misery which he and those with him were suffering, my passion burst forth in plentiful tears, which continued long and uninterrupted—relieving my breast, and perceptibly doing me a benefit my mind had languished for. This is what my poor father wrote :—

EDWINSTOWE, 17th August 1809.

O! my ever dearest Charles, how shall I find words to express all that we have suffered and shall suffer, till we hear the joyful tidings of your being quite out of danger? Thank the Almighty, all the accounts we have received confirm your dear letter, but still you know our hearts too well to suppose one moment of comfort can really possess us till every danger is passed. If anybody had told me you were to come home with the loss of a limb, it would have made me wretched. Now, it is all my hope and prayer—I see nothing dreadful in it. All the letters I have received from General Sherbrooke, from Stewart, and Colonel Fletcher give the most favourable accounts, and might content minds commonly affectionate.—I cannot proceed—may the God of all mercy send you safely to us. I have written to Mrs. Meynell to write to Admiral Berkeley; Lord Manvers has likewise written. God for ever bless and preserve you. With the most affectionate love of us all, I am, my ever dearest Charles, yours, with the truest love and affection,

W. BOOTHBY.

Draw on me for what money you may have occasion for.

The next letter I opened, being directed by my father, was from his angelic neighbour. I copy it :—

EDWINSTOWE, 17th August 1809.

MY DEAR CHARLES,—Your father is writing to you, and sends his letter to Lord William Bentinck, and I write this to send by another channel, through the Foreign Office. It is a great comfort to me to be able to give you a satisfactory account of your dear friends here; their anxiety about you is what you can easily conceive, but they look forward to seeing you return to us in good health, and their thankfulness that you have escaped with life keeps pace with their grief to hear of your sufferings.

They received your letter and General Sherbrooke's last night, since which we have scarcely left them ; your dear mother and Louisa are now composed, and your father also.   Louisa will write to you to-morrow ; the kindness of your letter has been a balm to them all.   We all join in prayers for your perfect recovery, and shall be most anxious for further accounts from you, and still more anxious to see you here.   Milnes and myself feel for you as if you were one of our own children, and partake of the distress of your family.   May God bless you, my dear Charles.   Brooke was from home on the moors, but quite well, and they expect him as soon as he hears of this disastrous engagement.

We shall devote our time to the comfort of your friends, till they have further accounts from you.—Believe me, my dear Charles, with every kind wish, most affection-ately yours,   CHARLOTTE MILNES.

Lord Manvers has written to Admiral Berkeley about you, and a friend of mine will also write.

How comfortable was this considerate and benignant letter !   At reading that which follows —from my brother — my tears fell in greater abundance :—

ISLE OF WIGHT, 18th August 1809.

MY VERY DEAREST CHARLES,—Let this but find you recovering !   I humbly pray to God that you may be re-stored to us.   When I feel secure of that, I will endeavour not to repine at the loss you have sustained—at the terms upon which we get you back.   Come to us, my ever

dearest brother, and allow us to watch over and tend
you ! You can come to us without any land carriage ; we
have a room for you, and the best surgical attendance.
It will gladden my heart and delight your sister to
alleviate by our warmest attentions your present situation. My kind friend Bathurst, in a letter dated the 31st
July, has communicated all you have undergone, and has
given an account of the general regret in the army at
your misfortune, with a tribute to your worth as a soldier
most grateful to me. I have written to our dear parents ;
therefore set your mind at ease, and only think of
gladdening us all by your arrival. Let us have that dear
recompense for the wretched anxiety we have within
these few days undergone. All belonging to you are
well, and when you are restored to them, will still be
happy. With what joy, if it please the Almighty to
permit it, shall I meet you at Portsmouth and convey
you to our abode, where everything will be devoted to
you ! I think it fortunate to be so near the coast; the
Isle of Wight will be the best place for you to recover
in, and we have a carriage, when you are able, to drive
you gently about in. Do come to us, my dear, dear
Charles ! Fanny and my children send affectionate love
to you, and of the truest love of your brother I need
hardly assure you. God send you a good passage to
Portsmouth. Adieu, my dearest lad !—Yours ever
most affectionately,   W. BOOTHBY.

These letters made me feel again of some importance in the world, and seemed to establish the
reality of my fond connection with it. My tears
ceased not to flow. My mind could not suffer

such a picture of my family's distress (which was
too easily visible to it) without some pain ; but,
though totally subdued, my heart was much less
affected than soothed and softened.

Had I needed a lesson on submission, the death
of a young officer of the Guards which happened
on the 30th of September might have read it to
me impressively. Captain Bryan had only a
mother ; she only a son ; and one of the fairest
graces of his all-gracious nature was the fondness
with which he loved that lonely parent. From
the situation of his wound, which was in the
thigh, amputation was impracticable. It was
deemed a dangerous but not inevitably mortal
wound. The hopes sent to his mother along with
the first disastrous news were probably as great as
those by which mine had been consoled. With
what ardour had my parents clung to those hopes !
But the widow — ah ! what but Heaven shall
pretend to support her when the bitter certainty
comes ? While she, with a heart sickly anxious,
is looking for the accustomed letter, her noble son
has mouldered in the ground. His only agony at
leaving life thus in its dawn was that with him his
mother's peace would sink for ever. "You see,"
he said to Higgins, "I don't mind about dying on
my own account ; but it's so dismal to think of my
poor mother. I am the only being belonging to
her—she is wholly wrapt up in me—and I much

fear my death will be hers. But it is not so dreadful to me to think of her dead as at the moment when she finds I am gone—for I fear she does not expect it." This young officer, whose kindly nature was fully attested by the love, the respect, and the deep regret of all his brother officers, was only known to me by the intercourse of reciprocal kind messages and good offices since our common misfortune. When he died, I could not help congratulating myself that I had known him no more intimately; nor could I, when thinking of his mother, not be grateful that affliction had pressed with a lighter hand upon those I loved—that not only had hope been suffered to soften their bitterest tears, but that my life had been spared to wipe them quite away.

Mine, therefore, at reading their letters were sweet and salutary tears; though Higgins, who came to me ere they had dried, deemed them the indication of a mischievous sorrow. For he, I think, was the person upon whose information my kindest friend, General Sherbrooke, wrote to my father as follows :—

BADAJOS, 24th October 1809.

MY DEAR SIR,—Enclosed is a letter from your son which came under cover to me, and was brought into the Spanish advanced post by a flag of truce. Captain Boothby sent me a few lines by the same conveyance,

dated the 13th. He was then quite well, and expected
to go to Madrid the day following.

It seems he has been very unhappy, at learning from
you the misery which his misfortune has occasioned his
friends.   Permit me to recommend, when any of you
write to him again, that this painful subject be touched
upon as slightly as possible, and that you should rather
signify the joy you feel at his recovery, and the very
sanguine hopes you entertain of soon seeing him again
in England.   I am induced to trouble you with this
piece of advice, having learnt from another person that
Captain B. was particularly low-spirited after he received
the last letters from his friends.

You will, I am sure, impute to its proper motive what
I am now saying.—With best compliments to Mrs.
Boothby, believe me, yours very truly—in haste,

J. C. SHERBOOKE.

I enclose also a letter for Lady Milnes.

On the day on which General Sherbrooke had
written thus to England, my poor Mulcaster addressed himself to me.   I did not get his letter
until I had been some time at Madrid.   I transcribe
it with a heavy heart :—

24th October 1809.

MY DEAR BOOTHBY,—I had yesterday the pleasure of
receiving yours of the 13th ; I had before heard from
Captain Christie of the Coldstream Guards of your recovery.   I have been officious enough to write twice to
your father, as good accounts of you reached us, when
General Sherbrooke was absent—it could do no harm,

and might be satisfactory. I am about to set off for Lisbon, where I shall probably remain some time. Pasley, who was dangerously wounded at Flushing, is fast recovering. There is no particular news, except that Mr. Canning and Lord Castlereagh, after having fought, and the former being slightly wounded, have vacated their places in the Ministry, which is not yet newly arranged. Fletcher is not with us at present; I shall send your letter on to him. We are all made happy by hearing of your complete recovery.

Burgoyne, Forster, and the little Scot join their best love to mine. That we may shortly see you, is the constant wish of your ever sincere and affectionate friend,

ED. RT. MULCASTER.

Aqueduct of Segovia (p. 215).

CHAPTER XVII

AMONG the letters which I received on the 13th of October were two from General Sherbrooke, written at an interval of several weeks, although they now reached me together.

As they tended very much to shake the resolution which Mortier's advice had a few days ago established in my mind, I copy them both as the best elucidation of the doubt they threw me into :—

15th September 1809.

MY DEAR BOOTHBY,—Yours of the 9th of August I received, and I forwarded the letter therein enclosed to your father immediately. Send me any other letters for your family or for any other of your friends, and I will take great care that they are sent to them. I have received a letter from my brother dated the morning of the 17th of August ; he had the night before received mine, informing him of your having been wounded, and he was then about to ride over to Edwinstowe to see your father. Your family were then all well ; any information which may reach me respecting them I will forward to you. Pray let me know whether or no there is anything you want, or if you would wish me to remit you any cash. The Commander of the Forces (now Lord Viscount Wellington in the county of Somerset, and Baron Wellesley of the Douro) writes me word that he is sending money to the officers who are prisoners. Perhaps this supply may furnish you with less than you want; if so, and you wish any in addition, mention the sum when you write to me, and the next flag shall bring it to you.

The new titles of the Commander of the Forces have not yet been announced to the army ; observe, therefore, that what I give you I take from the English papers, which may not be correct.

I hear that poor Colonel Donelan is dead. Of the other wounded officers we have good accounts. I conclude this will find you at Madrid, and that you will shortly obtain your parole. I don't know whether Generals Regnier or Maurice Mathieu may be with the French army in Spain ; if they be, I daresay they will recollect the exertions I made, at their request, to recover the liberty of two officers, who had been sent by the Sicilian Government to Pantellaria last year, when I commanded in Sicily. One was a Chef de Bataillon named Laborie ; the other, a Capitaine du Génie, whose name I do not now recollect.

But as I got them both released, and restored both these officers to the French army in Calabria, I make no doubt but, if either of those Generals are at Madrid, they will, in return for the good office I was so fortunate as to have it in my power to render to these their countrymen, do me the favour to exert their influence to procure you your parole. Remember me most kindly to Major Coglan, Captains Blair, Geils, Milman, and to all my other friends with you, and believe me, with much esteem and regard, yours very faithfully and truly,

J. C. Sherbrooke.

Captain Boothby,
Royal British Engineers,
Prisoner of War.

I am not at all pleased at what you call "*the caprice of your detruncated limb*," but recommend the greatest care and attention to getting it healed.   Unless you can effect this, you will not be able to travel, even if you obtain your parole, which I shall hope soon to hear has been granted to you.   The latest letter I have from Oxton is dated 28th August; your father and mother were then well, and had in some degree recovered their composure; for I need not conceal from you that they were at first very much afflicted, on hearing of your misfortune.   Attend, therefore, to your recovery on their account as well as on your own.   J. C. S.

5th October 1809.

My dear Boothby,—Many thanks for your very friendly letter of the 14th of September, enclosing one for your father, which I shall have great pleasure indeed in forwarding to him by the mail which I understand is to be made up to-morrow morning.

I hope you received a letter I sent you about three weeks ago, in which, among other things, I informed you that Sir Arthur Wellesley was created Viscount Wellington.   I will speak to his Lordship on the subject of your exchange, as you desire.   He is already well acquainted with my desire to get this effected, but I doubt whether it can be accomplished in the way you propose. Be assured, however, that I will spare no pains or exertions to obtain your release.

In my last letter to you, I mentioned some claim I have upon the Generals of the French army for attention to any friend of mine whom the fortune of war may throw into their hands, from having exerted myself, at the request of Generals Regnier and Maurice Mathieu, to get two French officers released from the Island of Pantellaria, and in which I succeeded with the Sicilian Government.

I am unknown to the Duke of Treviso, but if there be any officer of your rank, prisoner with us, about whom he or any other of the French Generals feel interested, I beg you will send me his name, and that of the place he is supposed to be at, and I will use all the influence I have to effect an exchange between you. In the meantime, I make no doubt but, from your being incapacitated from serving by the loss of your leg, the French Commander will be induced by motives of humanity to give you leave to return to your family in England on parole ; and in the event of his granting you this indulgence, I shall ever look upon it as a personal obligation conferred upon me.

I inquired in my last whether you wanted money. If you do, let me know, and mention how much, as I shall have great pleasure in supplying you. Tell me also whenever you think I can be of any use to you, and in whatever way. I have not time to add more than to say I shall deliver your message to General Stewart and your other friends.

Write as often as you can, and believe me, with the most sincere regard and esteem, yours ever most truly,

J. C. SHERBROOKE, Lt.-Gen.

10

Though, from what I understood of the tenor of my captivity, I did not now believe practicable the scheme of liberation thus zealously proposed to me, yet the proposal came in too authentic a form, and from too respectable an authority, either to be disused by me or slighted by the French Commander. I determined to show him the last of these letters (containing a message to himself), and abide by the advice which, after perusing it, he should give me. I had just put it in my pocket for that purpose, when Higgins called upon me. He came to tell me that, as some cash had been forwarded by Lord Wellington for the use of the officers at Talavera, the Marshal Duke wished to see those who were about to leave it. Accordingly, I repaired to His Excellency's quarters, and found there many British officers, some of whom I now saw for the first time—Mortier, of a good-natured, friendly demeanour, with papers before him, towering up in the midst of them. The man with the phaeton having declined a trip to Madrid, I had made up my mind to go in the waggon, and Stanhope had determined to be my companion; accordingly, he was one of the group upon this occasion.

"Gentlemen," said Mortier, "Lord Wellesley has written to the Duke of Dalmatia forwarding to him a quantity of gold for the use of you and your brethren. But as the majority of the officers,

prisoners of war, are at Madrid, I have thought it
better to commit it to the charge of Captain Geils,
who goes there to-morrow. He is, I suppose, aware of
the manner in which it should be divided, and will
leave for the officers remaining here the proportion .
they may be entitled to. I am sorry to find that
Captain Geils is still too much an invalid to come
here himself. Is there any one who will receive
this money for him ?"

Captain Stephens of the 66th came forward, as
the senior officer present, and received it ; Mortier
comparing the money with Lord Wellington's .
letter very particularly, and then taking Captain
Stephens's receipt.

· The Duke, first asking very kindly if I was in
want of more money than was likely to come to
my share, begged I would dine with him ; then,
desiring the names of the officers who would accompany the convoy to Madrid, upon Stanhope's
name being mentioned, he asked if he were related
to Lord Stanhope, and to an affirmative answer
returned that he had been acquainted with two of
the sons of that nobleman. Some letters too had
been sent to him directed to Captain Howard of
the 23rd Light Dragoons, who had gone to
Madrid. In giving these to Captain Stephens,
the Marshal asked, " Is this Mr. Howard any
relation to Duke Howard ?" (I forget what his
reason was for making the inquiry.)

There was among the English officers here
assembled a very general feeling of attraction
towards Mortier, because of the cordial manner of
affability which he adopted towards them.

When all this was arranged, I opened to the
Duke the doubt which General Sherbrooke's letter
had raised as to the expediency of proceeding to
France, and, putting the letter into his hands, I
pointed out the part referring to himself; which
having read—

"With all my heart," said he, "I would do
this if it were in my power. I wish you had made
application to the Duke of Belluno, who took
upon himself to arrange several exchanges which I
have since suffered to be carried out. But now
it is impossible. The business is transferred to
Paris, and there you ought to be—or nothing
will be done."

I was again satisfied, and, leaving his presence,
I communicated with Captain Stephens (to whom
I was a stranger) on our approaching journey.
We settled that it would be best for me to join
the waggon at Captain Geils's quarters at the appointed hour next morning, which to the best of
my recollection was five o'clock. I then returned
home, and employed the short time I had remaining in answering the various letters I had received.
The impression of my father's was still warm upon
my mind, and I wrote to him as follows :—

TALAVERA DE LA REGNA, 13th Oct. 1809.

I shut the door and gave a full vent to my tears as I
read your poor letter,—though I had been aware of all
your sufferings, this document of them afflicted my heart
most deeply, which relieved itself in copious tears. I
consoled myself afterwards with the reflection that other
letters have long ere this told you that all danger was
over and that I was reconciled to my loss. Your having
been kept in suspense for my life has (I thank God, who
brings good out of evil) reconciled you also.

The Duke of Treviso (who is one of the kindest-
hearted men I ever met with, and who has treated me as
if I had a right to his care and attention) having received money and papers for us, had the good-nature to
pick out sixteen letters for me, so that no time might be
lost in putting an end to my anxiety. Among these was
a letter from William, which melted me again ; a sweet
and most consoling one from dear Lady Milnes; one from
Lady Vernon, of old date, apprising me of Georgiana's
approaching nuptials ; one from Sir Brooke, offering a
cork leg ; and some most kind from General Sherbrooke
and other officers,—they opened my heart, and I read
them all with the greatest pleasure. I go to Madrid to-
morrow. It is now late, and I dine with Marshal Mortier
at five o'clock, so that I cannot write a long letter, as I
must take some notice of the many kind ones I have
received.

My dearest, dearest Father ! amidst whatever I have
undergone, it has been your affliction that has lain heavy
at my heart. Had I been alone in the world—or at least,
loved only by such friends as surrounded my bed—my
sufferings would have been light. But I knew that
you could not bear to lose me, and therefore shrank from

death, for I have no fear of hereafter—I thank the Great God, that I am full of confidence in His mercy, and think of appearing before Him without trembling ; but I tremble at the thoughts of your grief; and when I was on the ground, expecting to be trampled to death, the only exclamation I remember to have made was, " O ! my poor friends ! "

Don't show this letter ; people may suppose I write for effect—*you* know I write from the heart and in the spirit of truth.

I never had better health in my life ; my thigh has been long healed : I have some remains of pain, or rather disquiet, therein ; but this I have no doubt will go off in time, and it is not now enough to interfere much with my comfort, or at all with my sleep. I tell you this, which you may not like, that you may believe all I say besides. I give you my honour that I conceal nothing from you respecting myself. If you were to stand at my door you would hear me laughing and talking just as usual, in spirits just as noisy—and as you will often again hear ; for, to make the best of our bargain, we shall in all probability see much more of each other than we should have done had things not happened as they have.

If I ever have room to fancy that the loss of my leg has traced one furrow on the dear, dear faces of yourself and my mother, or has at all affected the happiness of any of us, then I myself shall cruelly regret it. But it will not be so ! Surrounded by all that is most dear to my heart, I shall feel myself happy in having bought at such a price a life of tranquillity and social enjoyment, in exchange for one that I have found from the first but little suited to my disposition. God have us in His good care.   CHARLES.

I answered all the other letters, and then proceeded to dine with the Duke. He received me with the kindness of an old friend, placed me next to himself at table, and after dinner, finding on inquiry that I was unprovided with tea, took care to supply me with an article which he knew in England ranked among the necessaries of life. On taking leave, he gave me a letter addressed to Marshal Jourdan, in which he recommended me strongly to the good offices of that Commander-in-Chief; repeating his application for my exchange, or for my early and commodious conveyance to France, in order to further an object so desirable for my unfortunate situation. In short, though sensible of how much a noble mind deems due to the unfortunate, I was at a loss to conceive how I could have deserved such kindness and aid from the Marshal Duke of Treviso as would in all points have become the affection of a near relation.

At five o'clock on the morning of October 14, I took my leave of the kind Spaniards who had endeared themselves to me by such essential services and generous attachment. They were all in tears; those who had seen the sorrow of the good old Pollonia might well have supposed she was parting with a son. Was it possible I should leave them without emotion? I shall ever remember them with gratitude and affection, and wish it may be possible for me to befriend them.

On arriving at the place where the waggon was loading, I found that our baggage was all piled in the middle part of it, and that a little cell, capable of seating two persons, was reserved at each end. The cell over the hind wheels was occupied by Stanhope and myself. We made it as comfortable as we could, by sitting on the soft packages containing our beds. The first cell was arranged in a similar manner by Captains Geils and Stephens, whose wounds required a wheel conveyance. This which we were about to travel in, however, was but little calculated to soften to the wounded the rigours of the road. It had no springs, and was rather a large box or trunk placed upon wheels than a carriage for the transport of living animals. The lid of the trunk (if I may so call it) we were enabled to raise or close by a perforated bar, which could not, however, be changed in its position without much trouble and external aid. Our friend Higgins, who was present to witness our departure, lamented the rudeness of the conveyance ; but, recollecting that we had not more than eighty miles to go, we the more easily made up our minds to it. It was with some difficulty, and not without great suffering, that Captain Geils was got into his place. His pain was visible to us in the distended veins of his forehead and the tenseness of his features ; but he made no complaint. The waggon drove off.

I had been able to preserve a horse which remained with me at Talavera, and he now carried my servant.

Towers, an officer of the Guards who had been shot through both ankles, also was mounted. Several other English officers who had recovered from their wounds, and with them Mr. Staniland, the artillery surgeon, accompanied this convoy on foot ; which was further increased by followers of all sorts belonging to the French army, who dared not travel a single mile without such powerful protection.

Waggon conveying prisoners of war.

CHAPTER XVIII

THOUGH the road was excellent, our position immediately over the wheels without springs made the motion so rough that we could notice our passage over the smallest pebbles. If to Stephens and Stanhope it was fatiguing, and to me painful, to Geils it was extremity of pain. I have never seen more acute suffering than this journey inflicted on our unhappy fellow-traveller. When, from some extraordinary smoothness in the road, his quietness made us hope that some little remission was allowed him, lively chat and laughter passed between Stanhope and myself. Either the country we were passing over was unattractive, or the nature of the waggon made external observation difficult : at any rate, we ignored the scenery. Once, indeed, with a crowd of varying sensations that held me silent, I perceived we were crossing the Alverche. I remembered well how I had felt—how all-complete in the elastic power of youthful strength—when last, with an eye of the keenest interest, I surveyed

this river; for it was when my General had
desired me to seek upon its margin a position in
which we might dispute its passage with the
enemy. We travelled until after dark; and, that
we might be more easily accommodated, our party,
consisting of ten, was divided into two messes and
lodged in two separate rooms. This arrangement,
adopted not so much for its obvious convenience
to both divisions as in compassion to the nervous
irritability of the suffering Geils (whom the clamour
of ten wounded masters and the clatter of ten
blundering servants would have certainly dis-
tracted), gave some umbrage, as if the captains of
the party had thus arrogated to themselves a distinction incompatible with the good fellowship
which we all owed equally to one another. But it
was surely natural that our travelling together in
the waggon should dispose us to live together, and
that Towers should join the party of Geils, his
brother-Guardsman. Indeed, the unpleasant feeling excited by our separation was so unreasonable
that I believe it soon subsided of itself.

From Talavera to Sta. Olalla, where we halted
the first day, is six long leagues, not much less
than thirty miles; and travelling foot's pace in such
a conveyance during about fourteen hours we had
found exceedingly wearisome. We were therefore
most glad of any refreshment and rest within our
reach, and quarrelled with neither the scantiness

nor the rudeness of our lodging ; for we had food
and wine, and every man had space on the floor
for his mattress.   Geils, too, from the misery of the
waggon now found comparative ease, and discovered a raciness of humour and kindliness of
character that soon made the paroxysms of
nervous agony by which his speech was often interrupted act more forcibly upon our nerves.   He
had a great fund of anecdote, strength of observation, and novelty of thought ; and while, in the
respites he could procure, he was engaging all our
attention, a knife or a teaspoon dropt on the floor
would break off his discourse by an access of
temporary frenzy.   His wounded leg being
soundly healed, the surgeons attributed this extraordinary protraction of suffering and the entire
loss of use in the limb to an injury done to the
nerve, referring the patient to the softening hand
of time as the only hope of relief.

As our journey for the morrow was to extend
to Navalcarnero, a distance of eight or nine leagues,
or at least forty miles, the appointed hour of departure was three o'clock in the morning, which
made it very difficult for us to secure any breakfast ; and the hurry attending that hot-water
repast gave many a pang to poor Geils, who
could not see the boiling fluid poured into the tea-
pot without suffering as if it were falling on his
leg.   Yet the action of filling a vessel out of a

pailful of cold water and pouring it back again,
which he continued constantly, was the only
remedy that seemed to have the least power over
his pain.

The second day's journey was longer and more
wearisome, and further carried into the night
than the first. We rested twice during the day,
and observed that the soldiers who accompanied us,
or were stationed at the places we rested at, dare
not forage in the vineyards under our view without a strong escort for their protection. They
returned with long poles on their shoulders, loaded
with grapes, a line of glancing bayonets moving along with them. The greater toil of the
second day was borne with the more spirit from a
sense that we had not much more to perform.
We figured to ourselves Madrid as the land of
liberty, where we should naturally be under less
restraint than even at Talavera. We quickened
time in laying plans for the comfort and amuse-
ment of our residence in the metropolis, and were
well assured that the Dons, into whose care we
should probably fall, would be zealous to lighten
our captivity and misfortunes by every resource of
which their city was capable. We knew that its
order had been but little disturbed by the events of the
war ; and Frenchmen of every rank and temper at
Talavera, praising Madrid as *une ville de ressource*,
had urged us to hasten thither, as if it could not

for a moment be doubted that we should be free to avail ourselves of all its advantages.

We were much provoked, therefore, with Stephens, who, though in other respects the most desirable of companions, whenever we were indulging ourselves on this topic, endeavoured to damn all our expectations by expressing his conviction that we should be closely confined. Not that he could in the least bring us to his way of thinking; on the contrary, the idea was too improbable to have been received, even on good information; but Stephens had none, and only gave us the gloomy speculations of his downright Antigallicism. We showed him no mercy. We could believe the French capable of the greatest cruelty where policy enjoined it; but here, as we apprehended, it would be perfectly wanton, and highly offensive to the Spaniards, whom it was their interest to tranquillise, to treat rigorously a handful of wounded officers who had suffered in the cause of Spain.

"Well," said Stephens,—"wait and see!"

"When we are jaunting about Madrid together, our arguments may be more persuasive!"

"I wish to God they may," he returned very drily.

"I suppose," said Stanhope, "there are plenty of hackney coaches in Madrid?"

"I hope so," said Geils.

"Of course there are," said I.

"Not," resumed Stanhope, "that I would give twopence for them for myself—except in wet weather."

"I don't imagine that our jaunts in Madrid will depend much upon the weather," said Stephens, with affected gravity.

"Why, you don't really think," remonstrated I—"you don't in your conscience believe, that they'll confine us to the house—do you, Stephens?"

"Perhaps," returned he, "we may have leave to take the air in the back-yard and peep at Madrid through an iron rail!"

"Ha! ha! ha! What a croaker! We shall be about as much confined in Madrid as in London!"

"Thereabouts!" said Stanhope.

"Very little more!" murmured Geils.

"Well," said Stephens, "wait and see! I think I know these chaps!"

We were not so weak as to surrender our judgment to the influence of such national prejudice; yet the perpetual croaking of Stephens cast a damp upon our pleasing speculations, which prevented their so free communication.

On the third day, poor Geils's sufferings were greater than ever; and now come in sight of Madrid, he entreated of us that we would stop the waggon, have him left in a cottage by the roadside, and, having procured his billet, send his servant for him in a hackney coach. We saw that his torments blinded him to the impracticability of what he proposed ; for, though all but Stephens fully expected to live in the city free and unmolested, we knew that it could only be after having given our parole to its military authorities. We therefore attempted to cheer our afflicted companion by urging the near conclusion of our journey, and the little while that his patience would be longer required. But here the drivers, now come in sight of Madrid, and no longer needing protection, keeping the stony centre of the road, set off at a round trot, which carried his sufferings to a height that took from him the power of complaint. In spite of our loud remonstrances, they slackened not their pace until they reached the city, whose bounds are compact and defined, not, as in other capitals, blended into the country by interminable suburbs. As we drove slowly through the fine streets of the Spanish metropolis, we regaled ourselves with the view of populousness and plenty to which we had long been strangers. The inhabitants and wealthy shopkeepers and mantled gentlemen, standing at their doors or passing along, gazed after us with the most evident anxiety, peering under the lid of the waggon, that, assured we were English, they might exchange a silent sympathy with our friendly coun-

tenances, and mark by the melancholy interest of
their looks and gestures their compassion for our
misfortunes, and their regret to see us enter their
city in a manner so little consonant to their affection for our nation, and the hardships we had
suffered for theirs.

This was the interpretation we made of their
manners at the time, and my after-knowledge of
those people enables me now to give it as matter
of fact rather than conjecture.

Biscayan Peasant (p. 260).

CHAPTER XIX

WE passed quite through the town, and traversing
an open space shadowed by avenues of tall trees,
and beautified by sculptured fountains, we soon
found that we were going through pallisades,
sentries, and other symptoms of military guard.
This appearance caused a sudden balance between
our hopes and apprehensions, nor had either time
to preponderate before, entering the quadrangle of
the Retiro, we had drawn up to a door under the
guard of a sentinel. The Adjutant of the place
was here ready to receive us, and showed us, ten
in number, into three naked rooms opening into
one another, all which, he informed us, were at our
disposal.

They smelt like a French hospital recently
evacuated ; there was no chair, no table, no bed,
no vestige of furniture to be seen ; and poor Geils
was writhing on his crutches, and asking piteously
for a chair.

"Damnation !" said the Adjutant, with the
impetuosity of rage, raising to his head both

hands, in one of which was a cane,—" damnation !
have patience then !   If you won't have patience,
you shall have nothing ! "

Geils was in too much real pain to be so
sensible as we were of this officer's brutality.   He
only gathered that a chair was not to be had, and
begged to be placed upon the floor.

But the rest of us, disdaining to converse with
a clown who appeared to be as remote from
common humanity as from the manners of a
gentleman, demanded to speak with the Commandant of the place.

A man of gentler manners and better aspect then
appeared, and by his demeanour made us think
that he was ashamed of the treatment we experienced.

" Whatever you may want, gentlemen," said
he, " we will do what we can to provide."

" There is, sir," said I, " a sentry at the door :
are we to consider ourselves confined to these
rooms ? "

Colonel la Fond bowed.

" We cannot then stir out of doors ? "

" Not without the Governor's permission."

" I am charged by the Marshal Duke of Treviso with a letter to Marshal Jourdan ; how, under
these circumstances, can I present it to His Excellency ? "

" Give it to me, and I will send it to him."

"But I wish, sir, to deliver it in person, if I may be permitted to do so."

"If monsieur makes application to the Governor, it is very possible permission may be given."

"Will you, sir, convey my application to the Governor?"

"Assuredly."

I lost not a moment in writing to General Belliard, stating that the Duke of Treviso had committed to my care a letter for the Major-General of the army, which I was particularly desirous of delivering to His Excellency in person; and I earnestly solicited the Governor's permission to do so. I sent this letter to Colonel la Fond, whose residence was close by, claiming the performance of his promise.

Thus we found ourselves, like a few scattered and way-worn sheep, gathered into a strange fold—leaning against the wall in different parts of the room, or lying on the floor. The disappointment was complete and great to all but Stephens: he stood collected, in the sullen and unwelcome triumph of a prophet, who felt the pressure of the evils he had truly foretold. As we ruminated thus disconsolate — regretting even the waggon we had left — a stripling of a remarkably handsome exterior and very gentle address, with a napkin under his arm and a clean white apron before him, came suddenly among us, and with

all the ease of French self-possession made us a
profound bow.   We all stared at this unlooked-
for apparition, and waited a while to see what it
would signify.   After a pause, and seeming to
resolve what quarter of the room he might best
address himself to, he told us that he belonged to
the restaurateur who lived close by, and had taken
the liberty to come to ask if he might have the
honour of serving us.

Never was a restored prince received by his
devoted subjects with a more undoubting welcome
than we now gave this messenger.

"Can you give us some dinner?" said I.

"Whatever you may choose to have, monsieur,
can be got ready in a quarter of an hour.   Please
you, I fetch the bill of fare?"

"But stay!" said I, "how can we dine without a chair or table."

"The aubergiste, for the pleasure of serving
you, will do himself the honour to send chairs
and tables immediately."

Away he flew.

This most convenient neighbour was indeed a
very great consolation, and dinner was at least
something we could look forward to with pleasure.

Wishing to discover (in order to remove) the
cause which polluted these rooms with so dreadful
a savour, we found that we had been preceded
by Spanish prisoners, who, not permitted to

pass the door, had left the attics in a most foul
state, and it had not been thought needful in any
manner to purify the building for the reception of
British officers.

Jean—for that was the name of our Jove-sent
Ganymede—soon reappeared, aiding others to carry
in a vast pile of chairs and tables, which with a noiseless dexterity he soon bustled into form ; and, as if
possessed of the lamp of Aladdin, in a moment
showed us a table covered with ample damask,
porcelain, and silver, which gave to the apartment
a very agreeable air of furniture and comfort.

Having received our order respecting dinner,
the Slave of the Lamp vanished.

Our jailors brought in a supply of boards and
tressels to lay our beds upon, and we quickly made
our lodging arrangements. Our quarters consisted
of a large room between two small ones. The
small room at one end was occupied by Geils,
Stephens, and Towers ; the other by Stanhope
and myself ; the large central room by the rest
of the party. Having done what was possible for
the purification of our quarters, and the refreshment
of our persons by water and clean apparel, we
watched with some keenness for the return of our
slave, who soon whisked in a well-dressed and
most comfortable French dinner, with brisk and
palatable wine.

The next morning, with equal facility and

comfort, we were furnished with an English breakfast.

But so large a party soon became insupportable to poor Geils, who begged that the former division might be restored, when he found how ill we received his proposal to dine by himself. His wish was immediately complied with, and thereafter five of us dined in Geils's room —a step which might now with more reason displease the rest, since, from the specimen they had had of his good-humour and spirit, they had felt the value of his society.

The sentry having refused egress to our servants, and thus a difficulty having risen in procuring water, I was glad of the opportunity to write a laconic remonstrance to Colonel la Fond, simply stating that, to persons in our infirm state, to be debarred from supplying ourselves with water was peculiarly distressing. Colonel la Fond, as I intended, was alarmed to find himself formally petitioned for *water* by his wounded prisoners. He hastened to us and expressed his regret that we should have had room to impute such a barbarity to the French.

"You are sensible, I hope, messieurs, that the harshness with which you are treated does not proceed from any want of respect to you, but merely from policy with regard to the Spaniards, whom, you must know, we cannot trust."

"We have not been able, sir," answered I, "to comprehend the policy you speak of—perhaps that may be our fault—but if the policy be just, might it not have been thought essential to soften a little the rigour of captivity to officers on whom the misfortunes of war have already pressed somewhat heavily? Could no confinement less wretched than this have been found, wherein our recovery might have been promoted by the blessings of air and exercise? Surely, monsieur, policy did not make it necessary to show us, who with difficulty can either stand or walk, into naked rooms, destitute even of a chair, and noxious with the filth of former prisoners!"

"Whatever inconvenience you suffer here," said Colonel la Fond, "I sincerely regret—I only execute the orders I receive; but you will recollect that your situation here is only for the moment; you are considered to be on the march to France, and will proceed with the first convoy, unless, in consequence of stating your ill-health, you have previously been removed to the hospital. I beg to counsel you, messieurs, whose wounds will render so long a journey at present formidable, to represent without loss of time that your situation still demands medical care. You will then doubtless be removed to the hospital, where you will receive the most indulgent treatment."

We thanked Colonel la Fond for his gentle

behaviour and kind advice, which we promised to reflect on.   But we had been counselled to leave Talavera for Madrid, and had lost much liberty by the exchange.

The name *hospital* was not alluring, and perhaps, when there, we might wish ourselves back ; yet the journey was indeed formidable, if to be performed in such a machine as had brought us hither, or perhaps in one still less enviable.   For Geils it was out of the question ; the wound of Stephens was still open, and inflamed by the journey from Talavera ; and I, from the same cause, was now suffering so much that even opium could no longer procure me repose.

While we thus balanced as to the course we should pursue, who in a moment should appear to us but my social friend Taylor of the Artillery, accompanied by Mr. Dormer of the 14th Dragoons !

The Commissary of War in charge of the hospital had made my friend suspect my arrival along with other English officers, and having, as a great indulgence, permitted a French soldier to conduct him to the Retiro, Dormer, remembering the vicinity of the restaurateur, got leave to accompany him, that he might give particular directions for a perigord-pie.   That there might be no misunderstanding in this latter affair, the landlady herself paid us a visit, and talked about

the seasoning and size of the pie with a manner
of the most easy and lady-like civility.

During this dialogue, Taylor, taking me aside,
advised me strongly to have myself removed to
the hospital, where he and his party had been ever
since their arrival; I should find myself as comfortable as could well be in a close prison; also I
should have good medical attendance, and leisure
to arrange my departure for France in the way
I liked best.

I had scarcely time to thank Taylor for
his friendly zeal, before, the sentry clamour-
ing for his prisoners, they were obliged to hurry
away, ere we could fully express how glad
we were to see them, or ask them questions
which crowded to our minds as soon as they were
gone.

The advice of Taylor decided Geils, Stephens,
Towers, Stanhope, and myself in favour of the
hospital; the others were determined to proceed
to France. One of them would, on Stanhope's
account, have endeavoured to accompany us, had
he not hoped to effect his escape. Afterwards, I
believe, he succeeded. This was Lieutenant Wylde,
the Adjutant of the 29th Regiment, to which
Stanhope also belonged; from which circumstance
he was more with us than any of the other party,
and showing a wish not to be separate from his
brother officer, and having won Geils (to whom on

that point we entirely deferred) by his most honest
and frank, yet very peculiar, demeanour, we invited
him to join our society, to which he became a
very entertaining addition.   Except in gentleness
of manner, he was a youthful Uncle Toby, all his
ideas seeming to be conformed to some military
pattern.   Perfectly regardless of our laughter, and
seemingly unconscious of it, he would sit with
his eyes fixed on the ceiling, audibly, in gruff,
blunt phrase, narrating or anticipating the
manœuvres of the negro tribes who spread their
winged forces over that snowy tract.   The
tortuous cracks and their minor ramifications
were rivers with tributary streams.   The many
discolorations of various shade were treated as
mountains, fortresses, and woods ; and he would
very seriously discuss the strength of position
favouring either army, and the probability of
their effecting the passage of the great rivers
which he considered to be meandering between
them.   Nor was it always in the power of very
substantial and corporeal evidence to dissolve his
reverie.   For at dinner, against which his own
operations were far from imaginary, he was
still the busy historian, and now and then the
vigilant opponent, of the many foraging parties
sent out from the insect armies above our heads.

"They've carried mustard-pot-hill though, I
see!" he would say as he filled his mouth.

" They mustn't keep that post, or they'll cut off our supplies ! " and then putting the black squadron to the rout, he would gravely help himself to mustard.

Thus he went on, tracing their flying movements through the whole topography of the table, from the Tureen Mountain to Table-cloth Valley, and only carrying their positions where they seemed too much to straiten his own cantonments.

Several days had elapsed, leaving unnoticed a second letter which, in default of answer to the first, I had employed Jean to convey to the Governor. And this determined disregard of all written petition decided me not lightly to part with Mortier's recommendation ; hoping that some channel might shortly offer which I should have less reason to suspect than the two I had recently employed. I should have judged more wisely if I had reflected that a letter under the hand and seal of a Marshal of the Empire, addressed to the highest officer in Spain, was quite sure of finding its way. Yet, though I had become perhaps overwary, I had less doubt of the letter's reaching the hands of Jourdan than dread of its being forgotten and disregarded—unless I presented it myself, in which case some answer must be given in order to get rid of me.

Staying yet some days longer at the Retiro, our dislike to it abated. In the perfectly free and

friendly intercourse of well-assorted minds, a flow
of good spirits from one kindled the glee of the
rest, and none could groan or sigh without the
sustaining sympathy of several kindly hearts.
There grows a bond amid such circumstances of
friendship not often known to those associated only
by the urbanity of good neighbourhood or the gaiety
of pleasure.

The industry of our servants had purified our
abode, and the aspect from our ample sash
windows was living and various.   The large
square before us, bounded by the courtly façades
and fane-twinkling minarets of the Retiro, enclosed
a scene of ever-changing bustle, and that armed
mouth was under our view which alternately
swallowed and disgorged all the military expedience
conceived in the headquarters of the kingdom.

Our restaurateur continued to supply us with
excellent meals—at an extravagant price, it is true ;
yet, as we all had money, we drove away care,
and, hoping for better times, were merry, in spite
of our wounds, maims, and rigid confinement.

In truth, I look back to these days, of which it
would not be difficult to make a melancholy
picture, without much recollection of mental uneasiness ; so greatly is calamity lessened by
participation, and so disposed are we to cheer
ourselves in actual distress by encouraging the
hope of better times.

CHAPTER XX

THE Convent of St. Francis, cleared of its monastic inhabitants, was used as a general hospital by the French in Madrid; and we who had avowed our present inability to travel were in a few days removed to that enormous building. We were out of conceit with our new abode before we had penetrated to it, for we passed to it by spacious floors covered with every shape of human suffering.

We would have glided quickly through this scene afflicting to all our senses, but that Geils—whose own sufferings were sharp enough to occupy all his thoughts—could with difficulty be got along, and the avenue between the feet of the wretched patients was too narrow for my crutches to be used without deliberate caution.

When we had gained that corridor appropriated to the use of the officers, we were greeted by Taylor and other fellow-prisoners, who were useful and kind in facilitating to us the manner of the place. For the most part, each officer had hitherto enjoyed a monk's cell to himself; but on our

arrival it was no longer possible to give such
liberal accommodation. Stanhope and myself, and
I think Stephens and Towers, became fellow-
lodgers, and we dined as heretofore in Geils's room.
The cells or small apartments constructed on the
exterior face of the building were very cheerful,
looking west on a very pretty scene, which com-
prised a near view of the gorgeous palace and rural
villa of the King, and at a distance the mountains
and towers of the Escurial. Under the end
window which lighted the corridor came the
garden paling of the Duke del Infantado, and
looking to the south it commanded the great
roads to Talavera and Toledo, the magnificent
bridge over the disproportionate rivulet, and
the stately avenue extending on its nearest bank
which begins the highway to Aranjuez. These
two aspects, therefore, were full of life and interest,
and threw upon us the best beams of the sun.
But there were cells also constructed on the interior
face, whose windows, of course, opened to the dark
and gloomy quadrangle, the area of which, like the
bottom of a well, could from its depth receive no
ray of direct light ; nor could any fall upon that
window in the first story through which both
Stanhope and myself drew air. Dank weeds concealed the pavement of the court, thickening round
the mossy parapet of the well in its centre, and
round the foot of those quadrangular walls, which,

rising to a vast height above us, kept their dark hue until they reached the point where the sun's beams could overshoot the opposite side. Geils's room, in which we dined, looked the same way ; and casting a thought almost of fondness on the cheerful scene we had left, we were soon almost regretting that we had not set forth on our journey, whatever might have been its evils, rather than suffer ourselves to be immured in so gloomy a prison, where on all sides we were surrounded by squalid misery and contagious disease.

On opening my eyes to the unwelcome gloom the morning after our arrival, I found I had been awakened by the entrance of a Spaniard, whose youthful age was almost concealed by a large cocked hat, and his cloak so worn as to conceal all but his eyes and nose.

He walked up to my bedside, followed by a troop of dirty Spanish menials, bearing burdens. Seeing that I was awake, he asked in stiff French, and with so careful an emphasis as seemed to demand a categorical answer, how I had slept ; and perhaps supposing from my countenance that I was more inclined to ask why my sleep had been broken than to tell him if it had been sound, he announced himself as a Spanish physician, who had voluntarily come forward from motives of patriotism to attend upon the English prisoners.

Upon hearing this, I soon brushed away the

sullen trace of regretted slumber, and with a manner of unfeigned welcome I expressed myself obliged to him and happy to see him.

I had nothing to complain of but a continuance of pain, which broke my rest, hardly ever leaving me, and not now, as at first, yielding to the effects of opium.

After some consideration, he said that I might hope much from camphor and time, an amalgam which he had hardly ever known to fail! Satisfied to end our conference with that pleasant conceit, he stepped up to Stanhope's bed, and, nothing discouraged by a very audible snore, mechanically began his inquiries.

" Et vous, monsieur, avez-vous bien dormi ? "

" What ! " said Stanhope, still asleep.

" Je vous demands, monsieur ! comment vous avez passé la nuit ? "

" What ! "

" C'est peut-être que la blessure de monsieur soit déjà guéri ! "

Still without stirring, Stanhope seemed to answer, " What ! "

The phlegm of the Spaniard was moved neither by those unsatisfactory answers, nor by my laughter, which from the opening of the dialogue I could not restrain ; and he gravely applied to me to interpret his object to my companion.

As soon as I could bring my jaws together,

which laughter had kept apart, I shouted, "Stanhope! Stanhope!"

Waking now, and starting up in the utmost
amazement, he fastened his widened eyes upon
those of the immovable physician.

Not aware that he had hitherto slept, and
having found French ineffectual, the doctor addressed him now in Spanish:

"Onde sta usted herido?"

Stanhope, through all his amazement hearing
my laughter, could not restrain his own; and,
keeping his eyes still fixed upon the doctor's, he
cried out to me—

"What the devil does the fellow want?"

His mirth increased more than ever; then,
finding it was at the expense of the physician, he
became sensible of its impropriety; and when, to
recover himself, he looked away from the grave
character he feared he was offending, his eyes fell
upon the greasy, grinning, gaping group by
which he was followed. He was therefore obliged
to hide his head and have his laugh out. Instead of being provoked, I was pleased to see
that now the doctor began himself to be amused;
and at last having ascertained the case of this
most impracticable patient, with a face of perfect
self-complacency, he swept away, with his oily
train.

I had in the course of the day the mortification

to find that one of the Governor's aides-de-camp had a few days ago inquired for a British officer, who brought a letter for Marshal Jourdan ; and now, in consequence (it seemed) of the mistake which prevented my being discovered, that Minister had departed for France, without giving me an opportunity to benefit by Mortier's recommendation.

The party with which Taylor lived, contained, besides Dormer, whom I have mentioned before, Captain Howard of the 23rd Dragoons, who had been shot through the lungs ; Sir William Sheridan of the Guards, badly wounded in the legs and still on crutches; and Major Coglan of the 61st, who was wounded at the same time as myself, and was not less beloved as a companion than distinguished as an officer. These formed the leading set, and enjoyed the privilege of dining in a small refectory instead of a monk's cell ; but they soon lost it.

The second night after our arrival Coglan effected his escape. He disguised himself as a servant, and, bearing a basket on his arm, walked unmolested through the French Guard ; and the same evening, disguised in the same manner, several other officers successively found means to follow his example. Their flight was of course immediately known to those who remained, and though it was quite sure to entail on them a more rigorous, perhaps a vexatious confinement, they could only admit a common sentiment of exultation at the first success of the fugitives, and anxiety for its completion.

The expected storm was not tardy.

The Spanish physician went his morning rounds. He administered at those beds which contained patients, but regarded not those which were empty —held himself unconcerned ; but Mr. Larreguay, the old French Inspector, in silent trouble hastened to Mr. Commissary Perron, who, in utter dismay, made his report to the Commandant de la Place, who instantly repaired to the guilty spot.

The Commandant was an old officer, whom the black feathers in his hat announced to us as a General, and he bore besides the most favourable form of French gentility. As his office made him responsible for the security of the prisoners, his countenance and manner expressed a severity excited by the Governor's rebuke. But neither that irritation, nor the being assailed by one of us with uncourtly railing in language only intelligible enough to convey provocation, could make him forget that he had to do with persons whom their rank, their distress, and still more his power over them, entitled to more than ordinary politeness and consideration, as well as patience and forbearance ; or provoke him to carry his new precautions further than seemed necessary to prevent the recurrence of evasion. Another mark of high

character in him was that though the innocent
physician was examined and threatened, and all
others who were connected with the hospital, no
attempt was made to discover from us the manner
in which our comrades had escaped ; and the precautions taken convinced us it was not suspected.
To narrow our range, and keep us under the
survey of the sentries he placed in the corridor,
the General deprived Taylor's party of the refectory ; and, although he considered a loud remonstrance against this hardship with infinite patience,
he at last decided that it was necessary. But
though his manner to us admitted not the slightest
disrespect to mingle with its displeasure, he spoke
with reproach of the fugitives, and seemed to impute some dishonour to their escape.

This brought from Howard, who spoke French
well, a spirited and very gentleman-like remonstrance :

"Comment! mon Général!" said he, "surrounded by your sentries, and forcibly confined to
this narrow corridor, can you talk of dependence
on our parole ? Treat us like persons of honour!
Leave us at large ; and then our word shall be your
security, which no temptation, General, could
induce any one of us to break. But when we are
in prison we think it appertains to you to look to
us ; to us, to regain our liberty if we can. Our
brave companions have done no more ; and surely

it is not just to cast on their flight any dishonour-able stain."

"Believe me, Monsieur l'Officier," returned the General, "I mean nothing disrespectful. I certainly did understand from one of your com-panions, who appeared to me to speak for the rest, that I might indulge my own wish to impose the least possible restraint upon you, relying that no advantage would be taken of my moderation; for it rested with me to answer for your persons, and without such an understanding I should naturally have made your escape more difficult. But if I misunderstood that officer, or if he did not speak the sentiments of the rest, I must now repair my former omission; and, whatever pain it gives me to aggravate the hardship of your con-dition, I must prevent your escape!"

And he repeated his orders to the sentinel to let no one pass into the refectory.

In answer to one of our complaints, "And can you think," said he, "that it is not harder for me to impose than for you to bear this little privation? Believe me, it is much harder; for no one can go beyond me in respect for the helplessness of a prisoner of war. We may do with him what we please. Can there be a stronger motive for treating him with kindness? He has a thousand claims upon all our charities! And, as far as personal aid can avail you, there is nothing within my

individual power that I am not ready to do for all
or any one of you. But in this case my duty is
very narrow. It is thought advisable—and that
such a thought was admitted you cannot regret
more than I do—that you should not be at large.
You are entrusted to me. The liberty of an equal
number of my own friends and countrymen in
England depends upon your safe custody. For
every one of you who escapes by my lenity or
negligence I lose an officer to France, and consign
a brother to protracted captivity. Thus if you
can give me no security in your forbearance, I must
seek it elsewhere. I have already incurred the
just reproaches of the Governor; but those, I do
assure you, did not give me half the vexation
inflicted upon me by the hard necessity of coming
down here to decrease the comforts of the unfortunate."

I could have taken this noble old General in
my arms, so just were his sentiments, and his
manner, though refined, yet so earnestly sincere;
but no sounds my feelings could have dictated
would have had a chance of prevailing over the
torrent of rapid, incoherent, and unreasonable
complaint which broke upon the General's mild
discourse; who, perhaps, from the scarcely intelligible language in which it was conveyed,
conceiving the speaker had not understood his
expressions, gave a shrug of imposed forbearance,

and having made his orders clear to the sentries, left us, followed by the audible thanks and praises of all who could understand his language, or appreciate his demeanour.

But, fearing he might again suppose that one had spoken for all, we entreated Mr. Larreguay (an old gentleman who executed his office of Inspector with great kindness) to convey to the General an assurance of the pleasure and thankfulness with which we had recognised in his conduct all that could best distinguish a brave and high-bred enemy.

Mr. Larreguay accepted this commission with great alacrity and some surprise, for it had quite, he said, oppressed him to see so good a man as that General put upon so ungracious an office. He assured us that the amiable old man had uttered nothing that was not amply supported by the general benevolence and nobleness of his life, which made him universally beloved.

This fracas was soon followed by the removal for France of a great many officers, including the party from which Coglan had withdrawn himself—an event which deprived us of much agreeable society, but at the same time greatly improved our comfort in point of accommodation. It was heavily impaired by the precautions which to the good General had appeared necessary, yet, in fact, answered no other purpose than to torment the

prisoners, and tempt them to practise again that
method of escape which he had failed to discover
or suspect.

The sentries now placed at our doors, according
to their several humours, vexed us by day with
wanton restraints, such as forbidding us to look
out of the window; and by night disturbed our
rest by their shuffling march to and fro, and their
whistling or singing, which our entreaties for silence
commonly redoubled. But these soldiers, perpetually changed, could not soon acquire a personal
cognisance of the officers under their guard, who,
retaining the privilege of sending their servants
into the town for provisions, could still, under disguise, substitute their own persons, at a hazard
which they were now more willing to incur since
to the hope of regaining their liberty was joined
that of evading the present rigour of their confinement.

Thus more officers escaped, and the Commandant, now assured that his measures had missed
the evil they aimed at, ordered every officer whom
it was possible to move to be instantly deposited
in the Retiro, and thence put in march for France
without delay. The removal immediately began.
The lame and the infirm were invited to provide
for themselves suitable means of conveyance, and
several of us hired berlins or hackney coaches.
Sir William Sheridan, still using crutches, had been

for that reason suffered to remain when his former companions were removed ; but now the plea of much heavier infirmity was not admitted, and he was already seated in the carriage which he had hired. Ours too was waiting. Those who could walk, the waggon for our baggage, and our servants,—all were assembled in front of the hospital, and only waiting our arrival.

We were all employed in assisting, cheering, and compassionating poor Geils, who was suffering inordinate pain. Hitherto time, to which he was referred for his chance of recovery, had only added to a morbid susceptibility which not only the slightest motions, but even sounds, could cruelly agitate. His sudden removal, joined to the notion that they would attempt to take him to France in his present state, had thrown his nerves into such irritation that his features, darkened and convulsed, exhibited an appearance of suffering really alarming. In this condition, sitting midway upon the great stair of the convent, he was observed with great concern by Mr. Larreguay, who heard us complain of the cruelty of moving our companion, and immediately desired he might proceed no farther. Then, going out to the place of assemblage, he discussed the matter with the Commissary, and that officer being a good-natured man, whose anger had now subsided, selected from among us those who, in proportion as it would be cruel on account of their infirmity to move them, had it less in their power to escape. There was in consequence remanded to the hospital a considerable company, which included the whole party I had lived with.

Sir William Sheridan went with the others that evening to the Retiro, and shortly afterwards to France.

We now took undisputed possession of the best and most cheerful rooms. Stanhope and myself, accustomed to be together, liked better to share a cheerful cell than to have the sole command of a dark one, whose gloom solitude would deepen. The largest and best was allotted to Geils, and he still permitted us to assemble in it by day. Thus, after some annoyance (and to Geils, pain), our plight was greatly improved by this brisk affair.

The loss of so many fellow-prisoners brought us a great accession of quiet and repose ; and less suspicion prevailing against us, the restraint upon us was slackened so as but little to trouble our retirement.

CHAPTER XXI

THE assemblage of British officers in the hospital, when first we joined it, was much too large to make acquaintance with each individual a consequence of our aggregation. Besides the party with which I found Taylor, and that to which I belonged, I remember rather names than persons, and of names not many. None appeared to want society. The community had divided itself into sets suited to the respective facility and comfort of all; and every cell, by the communication it held with others, seemed equally well placed with our own. All but one—on the gloomy side—near the door of which no officer was seen to loiter, and whence no sound of life came forth; yet there, in passing when the door for a moment opened, twice I caught a glimpse of a ghastly figure, at one time standing erect, at another stretched on a comfortless bed. The apparent misery would, I hope, have been sufficiently interesting, but extreme youth was also visible in this wretched object, clothed in the garb of a British officer!

On my asking why, amid circumstances so desolate, he should, as it seemed, be thus abandoned by his proper associates and by all the world, a story came out, which accounted for those appearances.

The inhabitant of the unfrequented cell was a young officer who, overpowered by his fears, had fled from the battle of Talavera, and seemed now to be dying of disease as well as despair. By the policy of abhorring a coward in the army, flight is made more dreadful than death, and doubtless great military good results from it; therefore the sentiment is right and wholesome. But individual misery unmerited is its offspring, too; and though its adoption in a particular class may be defended upon particular principles, it would be difficult upon general ones to rescue it from a charge of injustice. I shall not attempt to claim great praise or admiration for any character of man that is destitute of personal courage; without it no man can perform, or be ready to perform, his duty; and often I know the want of it proceeds from the prostration of a mind deserted by every worthy impulse. Yet it is not more certain that bravery may remain the only redemption of a character every way else detestable, than that virtue and ingenuous feeling worthy of being loved are sometimes united with timidity. Virtue predominant will carry the timid man through acts of valour.

Fear may betray the man virtuously inclined into
conduct that calls for general contempt.   Is it
said that, to the feeling mind, fear herself would
present disgrace as the supreme danger ?   This is
true, if the option were offered to the capable
judgment ; but in the breast of a timorous man,
her guidance is naturally suspended by that sudden
and overpowering danger from which then his
loosened fears propel him ; and not until clear of
the gushing blood and roaring fire,

> Which shook affrighted Reason from her throne,

can her return present to his agonised view the
miserable choice he has made in her absence, which
all too late he would die to revoke.   A docile boy
enters into the profession his friends have chosen
for him, ignorant that he is less fit than other
youths to brave its dangers, till a scene such as
strong minds only bear unshaken suddenly bursts
upon his feeble temper.   Obeying, perhaps, an
instinctive impulse to be relieved from the agony
of his fears, the power of thought taken from him,
he flies.   Ever after, though innocent of crime,
incapable of it, nay, perhaps an example of benevolence and virtue, he is turned from with looks
of horror and excommunicating scorn !   But many
are the cases of suffering humanity which, unmerited and unmitigated, are beyond all remedy
but the compassion of Heaven.   The soldier who

exposes himself, as becomes him, may be doomed
by his bravery to endless captivity, to slavery, to
a lingering life of bodily pain, through which the
voice of honour's applause would vainly seek him!
Yet not more for these sad contingencies, which
menace the brave, can man devise a remedy, than
for the pitiless disgrace which awaits those estim-
able men who, unconscious of their want of courage
to bestow the life they yet sincerely offer to their
country, have adopted the profession of arms.
The glory of that profession requires that scorn
should wave behind the coward a scourge more
terrible than the sword before him, and if blinded
by fear he heed it not, that all may see she waves
it not idly, let her merciless lashes pursue him to
the grave! Yet, so sensible that this should be
that we suppress the sigh and disown the tear which
rise for his sufferings, who would not seize every
peculiarity which seemed to offer the boon of an
exception? If quietly we may relieve him,
unseen by those whom our lenity could mislead,
shall we not fly with joy to do it? or if the
circumstances of the victim point on us the
commands of our Saviour in his behalf, shall we
not eagerly plead the paramount obligation of
religion?

Geils, Stephens, Towers, and Stanhope did not
hesitate whether this unhappy youth were to be
pitied and sustained, or left to perish, and they

desired me to offer him the services of our little
company.

Nothing could be more abandoned than the
state in which I found him.   As the noise of my
crutches roused him from the posture in which he
was lying, he presented to me but the shadow of a
human being, so squalid and bloodless.   His body
so barely alive, and his spirit already so utterly
crushed, that by the side of this hideous alternative
death had seemed fair in the eyes of cowardice!
His mind was the prey of shame and despair, his
body of a wasting dysentery, and want of attendance (for even his servant but sparingly waited on
a master left alone by his equals) aggravated that
disorder by making it as loathsome as it was
dangerous.   Feeling how little desirable it was to
cure the evils which afflicted the one, leaving the
other but the more alive to those which were in-
curable, he seemed to have given up all interest in
life.   Distrusting the unwonted voice of kindness
and consideration with which he found himself
addressed, and imputing it to my ignorance of his
story, he hastened to remove it, perhaps expecting
my indignant departure to follow his explanation.
But when he found that our purpose of kindness
and support had been consequent upon our
knowledge of his disgrace, that we inquired with
interest into the progress of his disorder, saw
his medicines duly administered, provided with

care whatever he might safely eat, by visiting him
often, ourselves enforced the respect of his attendant, and engaged one of the women to provide for
the fit comfort of his room, the poor youth soon
discovered again some value in life ; and seemed
to hope that, if officers of character could regard
him without abhorrence, perhaps, when out of
the army, contempt might cease to pursue him.
Thus, his thoughts having assumed a more cheerful cast, he acknowledged our good offices with
thankfulness ; and now, careful of his own recovery,
in due time got the better of his disorder.
Thenceforward we invited him to come amongst
us when he liked and freely associated with him,
and so did all the brave officers who came to us
afterwards from Talavera ; all being soon persuaded
that we need not in such a season, when mutual
suffering had more recommended to us the temper
of Christianity, adhere with rigour to those laws
of military society, which were wholesome indeed
for general observance, however unjust to individuals. Had we not dared to dispense with
them on the present occasion, perhaps ourselves
had wanted courage, as well as common humanity.

If any suppose, from my not mentioning the
treatment this youth received from other officers
whom I have named, that it was less kind, or,
assenting to the propriety of *our* conduct, infer
that *theirs*, if different, was less to be defended,

their conclusions are certainly very precipitate, and
to the best of my belief entirely erroneous. I am
ignorant whether much intercourse or none at any
time obtained between the officers we found in the
hospital and him in disgrace, but I think the
circumstances under which he must have been first
remarked by them would not have pleaded with
us for the same indulgence as those into which he
had sunk when we found him. He had made so
little secret of his failure as to acknowledge it to
Marshal Mortier.   It was known even to the
enemy, and his own desire of seclusion was such
that, carefully avoiding the sight of any officers
belonging to his regiment, his choice was to be
surrounded by those who knew of him nothing
but his shame. For to be deprived of the power
of making new acquaintances, though solitary,
amid numbers, was a mortification many degrees
less than to meet at every turn the bleak eye of
averted friends. If, then, complying with his own
bent (which indeed best became one amid such
circumstances), those strangers left him to himself
unmolested, but unnoticed, I think they judged well,
and acted not unkindly.   And accustomed as they
would thereby be never to see him, except just
shutting himself into his cell whenever they entered
the corridor, the ailments of his body might well—
and I have no doubt did—advance unknown to
any of them.

His disorder was at first slight.   The physician
visited him as well as the rest.   He was in other
respects not worse provided, and his pitiable state
was, I believe, entirely unsuspected, until an
accidental observation betrayed it to us.   I find
by the dates I have preserved that the events I
have touched upon since our arrival at Madrid
occurred in so few days, and that the officers we
found in the hospital were so soon swept away,
that I cannot wonder I know so little of the
extent of their intercourse with this unhappy
young man, or the information they had of his
illness and despondency.   But my thorough conviction of the manly kindness and generosity of
their character, makes me feel perfectly sure that
either they showed kindness to him, or that if
they did not, when with propriety they might,
the opportunity was never made known to them.

I have before observed that since the removal
of the more active prisoners, being less suspected
of a purpose to escape, we were less vexatiously
observed by the sentries.   But this amendment
was perhaps more owing to the occasional presence
of the officer on guard, who, if it happened that
he had some gentleman-like feelings, gave us now
a good deal of his company, and by that means
expunged from the minds of the soldiers that
tendency to insolence which their authority to
control us had too readily excited.   Unless he

had been personally very disagreeable, his visit was sure to be welcome; for, having yet received no other, his throat was the only channel through which the town talk could reach us. On 25th October, however, a strange but very sharp-looking officer, most fancifully dressed in a sort of Mamlone garb, and smoking a long serpentine pipe, which hung dangling from his whiskered lips, came slashing up the corridor reiterating my name.

On my answering to that random call, he said he was desired by Marshal Mortier to wait upon me, to see if I were comfortably situated, and to offer me freely both the Marshal's services and his own. I was greatly pleased with this mark of kind remembrance from one who by his former extraordinary goodness had commanded my affection, and I asked warmly after the health of the Marshal Duke, and if there was any chance of his coming to Madrid. Monsieur Galabert (for that was his name) answered that not only had he the satisfaction to assure me he had left him in perfect health, but also that His Excellency was daily expected in the capital, and in the meantime, he begged to reiterate his offers of service.

We learnt from this officer, who was very loquacious and self-confident, that Soult was appointed Major-General of the army in the room of Jourdan, who only waited to give up the charge.

"I suppose, messieurs," added he, "you know that General Wellesley has embarked at Cadiz?"

"We knew no such thing," we said, "nor [laughing at him] did we believe it."

"Eh! comme vous voulez, messieurs!—vous êtes les maîtres!—but I solemnly assure you it is true! There is not at this moment a single Englishman upon the Peninsula, except as a prisoner, or perhaps in garrison at Cadiz. Your nation now confines its succour to advice and material; so that now our efforts are near their accomplishment, nor will the Marquis Wellesley, who is arrived at Seville, and it is believed will be named Regent, be able to retard it, however great his talents. That he has great talents few know better than I. I went to India to look after him, and in spite of his vigilance sent home the information desired! Si! si! Je le connais bien!"

"Then," said I, "you will be able to tell His Catholic Majesty what sort of a man he has to deal with!"

"Yes," returned he, with a sapient nod. "Yes, yes! I have already told them they must prepare to cope with a man of unbounded resources! But those are not enough without resources which are beyond his reach. Against French troops he must have at least an equal number of steady regulars. Spain cannot furnish them; and England has even recalled those she had furnished. For, indeed, you may rely upon the fact, gentlemen, that General Wellesley has embarked his army."

We told him, with something like a sneer, that people were apt too easily to believe what they would ardently desire; and that for our parts we confessed ourselves rather incredulous of news we disliked, and therefore trusted he would excuse us. Monsieur Galabert displayed a little national insolence and gasconade; but as he did not lose his good-humour on being rallied in turn, and rattled away in a style somewhat novel and entertaining, his visit was not only welcome to me from the kind messages he bore, but rather enlivening to all the party.

When he took leave, he mechanically discharged a profusion of gallant offers which he desired might be received, as they were made, *avec toute la franchise militaire.* His gold-bonneted head thrown back, his hands and whip thrust into the distended pouches of his immeasurable trousers, away he brushed at a five-mile lounge.

CHAPTER XXII

THE Duke of Treviso arrived at Madrid on the 26th of October. I wrote to him describing my situation and returning his own letter to Marshal Jourdan, which, I told him, I had not been allowed an opportunity to deliver.

He returned me a prompt answer, expressed as follows :—

26th October.

The Duke of Treviso has just received Captain Boothby's letter. He will see the Governor this evening, and he hopes that to-morrow Mr. Boothby will have free egress ; for the rest he may reckon on the endeavours of the Duke of Treviso to procure him all the indulgence his situation demands, and he will have the pleasure to see him to-morrow morning. It is to be wished that Mr. Boothby had sent direct to the Marshal Jourdan the letter addressed to him.

And it now seemed to me very odd that I had not done so. Nevertheless, my kind protector's note gave me no small satisfaction. It seemed even possible that he might now find some means of forwarding my return to England.

The next morning the officer of his guard arrived, and, asking for me, said he had the Governor's orders to accompany me to the Marshal. I apprehended, I said, His Excellency's residence might be at a greater distance than it would suit me to walk, and therefore begged the officer would wait until a carriage was procured. As we were proceeding together, the officer adverted to the Duke's disposition to befriend me, and the claim I derived from my misfortune.

" The Duke's opinion," said I, " is that if I could obtain an interview with the Emperor, he would immediately send me to England."

" He would," said the officer, " not because he would feel for your situation, but that he might seem to feel for it. It is thus that he has often done beautiful acts which narrate well ; but he feels for no one ! "

The Duke received me as he had parted from me, and continued to give me proofs of the most generous interest.

" I am going," said he, " to dine with the King, " and I will ask him to grant you your parole to go to Paris. He will probably not refuse me this favour, and then I will take you in my barouche as far as Valladolid."

I had no words to express my sense of this kindness, nor have I now.

Although he was to dine with the King himself,

he hoped I would dine with his officers. He could not, he said, interfere with the arrangements regarding the British prisoners in Madrid. He could not understand it. He had answered for me to the Governor this day. And he hoped soon that the King's compliance with his request would relieve me from every restraint. I reminded him of Captain Geils and his continued affliction, and said that he had been recommended some prepared baths, whose efficiency his confinement prevented his trying. And I entreated the Duke's good offices to have him lodged in the town. The excellent, the honest, the noble Duke promised to mention his case to the Governor Monk.

During the absence of their chief, the officers of Mortier's staff were much more easy and babbling than in his presence. They talked of the Treaty of Vienna, which made France indisputably the great nation. Russia, said one with a most profound countenance, may have more territory ; but it cannot be counted, it is so distant and so barbarous. "Non! en Europe, c'est bien la France qui soit sans contredit la grande nation !"

Seeing me smile, he immediately bowed and added—

"Je ne parle pas de ces messieurs. Ces sont les dieux de la Mer. C'est toute autre chose !"

I thought that a good trait in the man.

As the Duke had not said when he was likely

to go to Valladolid, I thought it best to prepare immediately for departure. I was in some difficulty about my servant, as my horse had been stolen, and I did not know how in so short a time to provide for his journey. At the worst, I thought it would not be difficult, with Mortier's assistance, to contrive that he should follow me.

Notwithstanding the brightened hope now offered to me, by performing so commodiously much the worse part of the journey to France, and for the remainder having the aid of that powerful friend who would there be in command, it gave me much pain to think of parting with my companions, more especially when I saw the regret which gave a melancholy tone to their sincere congratulations.

Until the 30th of October I wondered what could prevent my hearing more of Mortier, but we then from the corridor window saw that Chief, accompanied by his staff, proceeding over the bridge and retracing the road to Talavera. I readily supposed that some military charge had recalled him to that quarter instead of sending him to that of Valladolid, and at once conceived that to me he could not with propriety advert to any such change. While we were accounting for what we beheld, an officer arrived with the following note:—

29th October.

SIR, — His Catholic Majesty has been pleased to permit you to repair to Paris on parole, to take the orders of H.E. the Minister of War relating to your exchange. The Marshal Jourdan will send you the written authority to-day or to-morrow. I am charmed to have been able to be useful to you, and wish you, sir, a happy journey.   THE MAR. DUC OF TREVISO.

Imperator.

CHAPTER XXIII

MADRID, *Wednesday, January* 10, 1810.—Having
passed a turbulent evening in the midst of harness,
turkeys, papers, hams, and pots of mustard, I
sleep with the fear of not waking—call Delacourt,
who reluctantly rises. We stir ourselves up with a
long pole. At half-past six set off in my own
chaise to the Retiro, having despatched a coach
for Stephens and Morgan to the Franciscan goal ;
these arrive soon after me. Breakfast at the
restaurateur's (our old friend) on *bœuf à la
mode, little birds*, and *café au lait*. The place is
filled with every description of French military,
who, preparing for a long, painful, and perilous
journey, have fortified their bodies with rude
dresses, regardless of the grotesque appearance
they make, wearing their cocked hats over red,
blue, and green nightcaps. My friend, who talked
English to me at Belliard's, comes up and most
cordially greets me ; he tells me that I have a
charming equipage, and that as my party
consists of three only, it happens extremely

lucky, as he himself will be happy to take the fourth seat!

"There is not a fourth seat, my good sir."

"'Tis an unhappy misfortune, my dear," returns he, more disappointed than piqued.

It is very ill-judged of my young friend Pakko, who breakfasted with us, to insist upon going part of the way with us, though we are already full; I have much ado to prevent Morgan from convincing him how much he is *de trop*. Stephens exults much at the success of my arrangements, and is delighted with the carriage. We shall be more at ease in rear of the convoy than in front. As we wind along under old St. Francis, we shoulder forward to look at the well-known window, and discover the rest of our crippled brethren looking out for us. We wave our handkerchiefs, but they do not answer the signal, probably not supposing we could inhabit so smart a vehicle.

Travel through a disagreeable hilly country— few villages, those desolate. The convoy is conducted by a Chef de Bataillon, an active little savage. The bayonets are about 300, escorting English and Spanish prisoners; six or seven caissons, with sick French officers; bullock-carts with sick and maimed of all nations, and several coaches, berlins, and cabriolets, which have taken advantage of the convoy's protection, from fear of those predatory Spaniards whom the French call

brigands—I believe they molest and rob Frenchmen only. About eight o'clock at night we bring
in sight the village of our destination, Calapajar,
five long leagues from Madrid. We know by the
crashing and blazing in the village that the French
are preparing for supper at the expense of the
doors, windows, and furniture of the unfortunate
Spaniards.

We enter the town, and are told that the orders
are to lodge *militairement*. We are warm in the
carriage and have victuals. As many of our comforts depend much on the outside passengers and
horses, this lodging *militairement* we by no means
approve of. So getting out of the chay, and
crutching through the turmoil, we find our way
to the Commandant of the Place, and beg he will
order us a lodging, saying that we are English
officers. He begs us to come in, and desires the
Alcaldy to give a billet for three officers. The
Alcaldy turning to me says in Spanish, " For three
officers, sir ? " I answer in his own tongue, " Yes,
sir, for three English officers." English ! repeat
the surrounding Spaniards (surprised and suddenly
affected, as they look at my crutches and little
Morgan's empty sleeve). " My God ! they are
English officers ! " They say no more ; a dead
silence prevails, until the French officer asks me
if I myself am not a Frenchman. " No, I am an
Englishman."—" That is," returns he, " you

serve with the English, but you are French by birth ! "—" Pardon me, sir ; I am a legitimate Englishman."

We are sent to a miserable house, but some Spanish women follow us out of the Commandant's house, and when we come to a place where no one can observe us, they stop us, burst into tears and lamentations, and, with all the frensical vehemence of long-smothered enthusiasm, clasp us in their arms and imprint our faces with kisses of agony and tenderness. Then, sobbing and wringing their hands with a poignancy of grief almost maternal, they suffer us to proceed, and give themselves to despair. Had the motive of this rare burst of virtuous sentiment been less sacred, the scene less impressive, or events we had witnessed less fresh upon our minds, perhaps this adventure had excited us to mirth. Far different are our feelings. Every tendency to compassion is moved within us. Affected beyond measure, and struck with the highest admiration, far from forgiving any thought of levity, I should be angry with that man who, dry-eyed, could have beheld the surprising conduct of those patriotic women. On entering the house the billet indicated, we find it preoccupied by four French soldiers, and hardly have time to growl at this nuisance before the Alcaldy, having despatched his business and then followed us, takes us with him to his own house, where all his humble means are put forth to entertain us. Spreading our beds on the earthy floor of the inner cabin, we open our hampers, and having set out an admirable piece of spiced beef, a huge cold turkey, and a great leathern bottle of Madeira, we invite our rustic host to partake with us. In this honour he will suffer none of his household, not even his wife, to share; but carefully closing and securing the door, he sits down with us more from curiosity than appetite, and anxiously asks for all we know of the affairs of his unfortunate country, and whether there be any chance of freeing her from the legions of the devil.

Friday, January 26, 1810.—Rise by candle-light, contrive to get a little hot tea, and, thanking the good Alcaldy, start. See, by the way, that our savage commanding is a most irascible animal. Pass over a not unpleasant country—weather beautiful. The road passing into the wild mountains that toss their rugged heads about the lordly Escurial becomes strewed with bloody skeletons and mangled carcases of men, murdered and buried by the road-side, but again raked up and half-devoured by the ravenous wolves that infest these mountains. No sight can be more revolting to humanity: it realises the bugbear of children, *raw-head and bloody bones*. The gaiety of the sunbeams glistening on the snowy mountains, and the courtly beauty of the Escurial, dissipate much of the horror. The very steep mountain, which traverses this day's march, proves the mule a stout heart and the mare a *coquine*, unequal to her share of the draught. We fall into rear of the convoy. Stephens and Morgan walk on the edge of the precipice on the right hand. A bullock, rendered mad by being driven though lame, runs at them, and, as they turn to run, with his horns at Stephens's back precipitates him ! I lose sight of Stephens ; but, rising in the carriage, I see him lying at the bottom of the steep without the smallest motion or sign of life.

Soon, however, he comes to life, but not to recollection, and for more than a quarter of an hour after being put into the carriage exhibits the horror of a struggle with mental derangement. He mends, however, and soon is able to walk again, which refreshes him much. I am now obliged to walk too, to lighten the carriage, and we begin to be alarmed about getting up the hill. At length all our efforts are vain ! The mare will stir no more. Just now a carter, with a convoy of hay drawn by bullocks, meets us. I invite him to help us up the hill ; seeing the soldiers with us, he assents, and all his pairs of bullocks are pressed by them. I beg the soldiers that when they come to the top they will let him go. They say yes. He puts on his bullocks before our cattle, and so awkwardly that at the first start down comes the mare. The oxen then draw us up very quietly—

draw us up alone.   Come to the top, he demands
to go, but the soldiers are deaf.   The peasant appeals
to me; I intercede; but the Frenchmen oppose the
order of their Commander.   I tell the man that I
have no authority over them ; he offers to take us
to Otero if I will set the rest of the oxen free.   I
still plead want of power, and we proceed—down
the steep descent, with a stupendous precipice without the slightest fence on the right hand.   Suddenly one of the bullocks begins to kick with fury,
and dart about in a terrible manner.   In full expectation of dashing down the immeasurable steep,
I hastily order the door to be opened, and the
servants help me to jump out.   I revile the peasant,
who, we were all persuaded, had whispered to his
animal to set a-madding, out of revenge.   His
beasts are unyoked, and down he goes in
triumph ; with difficulty we follow with our
own, for frozen snow, forming an icy slope, makes
the road most perilous.   The road descends
suddenly, and the scenery is greatly romantic.   At
the foot of the mountain we meet the malicious
old peasant returning with his bullocks, and he
asks the reward I promised him.   I shake my fist
at him and give him nothing, while Morgan abuses
him in very good English.

   We find the rearguard with the bullock-carts
at halt at a post consisting of a large building and
a church, where the grand road, I believe, con-

tinues *right on*, and the road to Segovia, or the *route d'Étapes*, inclines to the right. It is getting dusk, and without much reflection we continue alone our way to Otero, now distant two leagues. It soon falls dark, and we observe the road, heavy and well-bushed, is very favourable for brigandage. We meet a man and ask the distance ; he answers one league and a half; and, as we go at a brisk walk, we settle our arrival at an hour and a half. The moon rises. We dread the slightest hill on account of the mare. The time having elapsed, we look about for the village in vain, and see with consternation a most serious hill before us. The road is very heavy. With utmost exertion, and all hands afoot, we get half-way up and there stick. As the town must be close by, we think it best that Stephens, who complains of the consequences of his fall, should mount his grey pigmy and, accompanied by his man Reynolds, proceed to the village and request assistance from the Chef de Bataillon. I write a note on a leaf of this book by the light of the moon that

Shadowy sets off the face of things.

Stephens and his man start. Morgan and myself getting into the carriage, and drawing up the glasses, compose ourselves for a nap, while the warmth of gallantry for Reynold's bride prevents Aaron Delacourt, my man, and Moses Parnell,

Morgan's, from minding the frost, the snow, and the keen wind; and I am willing to hope that the bright flame of chastity is equally serviceable to the Square Lady! No sooner is Stephens gone than I discover a league-stone, which tells me, by saying 10 *L. from Madrid*, that it wants yet a league to Otero; so that Morgan and myself make up our minds for a considerable time of perditage. Soon, by the sound of voices that cheerily break through the stillness of the night, we are apprised that the rear of the convoy, which we had passed at halt, is approaching. When they come up to us and find us hopelessly sticking there, the French soldiers make very much a concern of our distress, and insist upon shouldering the wheel. This expedient failing, they leave us with regret and terror, one of them assuring me that he would speak to the Sergeant to send back a pair of oxen to drag us up the hill. So once more we are left alone among the robbers. We hand out a cup of Madeira to each of the outside passengers, and compose ourselves again to sleep. Let those who hold that distant dangers are less terrible say why, at Madrid, we felt enough of apprehension about the brigands to make us dislike the journey, and now in the midst of their haunts, and at the dead of night, alone, we feel no sort of alarm; for

Evils dreaded are ten times as great
As when they press us with their actual weight.

From the first, I never should have thought of
dreading any intentional injury from these brigands;
but as their mode of attack is naturally firing upon
the convoy from their lurking places, as it passes
through strong country, and never showing themselves till half are killed and the other half in
flight, the goodwill of our friends might have
come in action too late.

After waiting an hour in this situation, to our
surprise a party of French soldiers appears with the
promised bullocks. These good fellows express
the utmost joy at finding us safe. They yoke-to
the oxen, which immediately begin to dart about
like mad bulls, whirling the carriage round and
round. Morgan and I clamour lustily to get out,
and in a pause descend. Now we hook the kindly
mule in front, which obligingly undertakes to draw
a full third, and up we get at last. At the top
of the hill the Sergeant says he would willingly
give us the oxen on to the village, but cannot, as he
has taken them from a cart occupied by wounded,
whom it is impossible to leave upon the road. He
may say that! So once again we are left to our
own beasts, who go on very well until just near
the entrance of the town, where (having passed a
wild of rocks rather than a road) the carriage
obstinately sticks in a huge hole, and the mare

will not even try to get us out ; so I leave Morgan,
and hobble cautiously on my crutches—difficult
from the dark and roughness of the way—and
seek the Commandant of the Place. The village
is in good order. The Commandant is very
friendly, and sends his servant to find Stephens's
lodging ; and in the meantime we sit down to sup
on cold mutton and salad. When the man comes
with the direction for the billet of Stephens, whom
I had greatly feared to be lost, I follow him. The
streets consist of the untamed rock. "How the
devil, thinks I, will the berlin get over all this ? "
But entering the premises I see a carriage in the
yard : so I think, again, that where one has come
another may. How is my satisfaction increased
to recognise, on a closer inspection, my own venerable berlin !

From this point the luck seems to change ; I
find everything in clover. Morgan and Stephens
sit by a rare kitchen fire preparing for supper.
We sup lightly. The good people of the house are
loving and characteristic. We are tired and ripe
for sleep—hardly can I resolve to write another
word. Thus well has ended this disastrous day,
and the pleasures of a comfortable port are much
enhanced in reflecting on the gales and buffetings
at sea !

Otero is six long leagues from Calapajar.

Friday, January 12, 1810. — Get up, eat a

good breakfast, get two bullocks to put before
our mules, and set out walking—delightful morning. Pass the Palace of *Rio Trio*. It reminds us
of Thoresby—a colossal statue of the House at
Thoresby, in a barren plain. Immense steep hills,
but the good, docile bullocks draw us up apparently without exertion. See a palace of the King
at the foot of mountains on the right, where he
was wont to repair to cool himself in summer.
'Tis the Palace of St. Ildefonso. Arrive at Segovia
at half-past two. An old wretched town in a bare,
rugged country, has old turreted walls, no good
buildings, but a beautiful, venerable aqueduct, consisting of two tiers of arches in the style of the
bridge of Alcantara, but indeed less grand and
striking. This only is worth seeing in the place.
Here we buy another mule, which we hope will
smooth our difficulties. In answer to an application from me for assistance of bullocks comes,
when I am in bed, an answer from the Chef de
Bataillon, couched as follows :—

À Monsieur Ch. Boothby,
    Capitaine Anglais, à Segovia.

Séjour demain.

MONSIEUR LE CAPITAINE,—J'ai reçu votre lettre et
vous préviens que vous pouvez être tranquilles sur la
demande que vous me faites ; du reste, je vous engage à
vouloir bien recommander à vos soldats prisonniers de

rester tranquilles, et de suivre avec ordre le convoi ; s'il en était autrement, je cesserais d'avoir les égards qui sont dus à votre rang.—J'ai l'honneur de vous saluer,

LE CHEF DE BATAILLON.

From the *Séjour demain* we are happy to find to-morrow is a halting day. I read the letter to Stephens and Morgan ; and then, dismissing the orderly and putting out the light, we confer on the contents from our several kingdoms. We think by any counsel of ours to impede the escape of our brother prisoners would be unworthy conduct, and therefore at once determine against it ; but, on the other hand, we know ourselves to be at the disposal of this *farouche* Colonel, and that it is well in his power to harass and torment us. To take no notice of the observation, as it does not demand an answer, might be best. But then he will suppose we admit the reasonableness of his expectation, and in case of any escapes, he would be emboldened to treat us with vigour and disrespect. It is best, therefore, to protest at once against the idea, and in a tone which, though respectful, shall give him to understand we will not be put upon. Here the council breaks up.

Saturday, January 13, 1810.—Write to the Chef de Bataillon as follows :—

SEGOVIA, *le* 13 *Janvier* 1810.

MONSIEUR LE COMMANDANT,—J'ai reçu hier au soir la lettre que vous m'avez fait l'honneur de m'écrire, et je vous rends les remercimens des officiers Anglais pour vos assurances des secours. Mais, je suis fâché, monsieur, qu'au même temps vous exigiez d'eux ce qu'ils croient ne pouvoir pas faire.

Il est peu nécessaire de vous dire que quand les soldats prisonniers sont tenté par l'espérance de retrouver leur liberté tout conseil que nous les donnassions ne les empêcherait de se sauver tous les fois qu'ils en trouvassent l'occasion, et qu'il ne soit pas possible de les empêcher qu'en les gardant, ce que ne tient qu'à vous.

Quant à nous, j'espère que vous nous feriez la justice de croire que l'engagement que nous vous ayons donné ne soit la garde la plus forte dont vous pussiez vous server.

Nous sommes bien persuadés que vous, Monsieur le Commandant, ne cesseriez pas d'avoir les égards qui sont dus à notre rang que quand nous aurions fait quelque chose qui en soit indigne.—J'ai l'honneur d'être, Monsieur le Commandant, votre très humble et très obéissant serviteur, CHARLES BOOTHBY,
Capitaine au Corps de Génie de S.M.B.

We walk about the town and dislike it more and more. The 28th Regiment enter from Astorga. Meet a fellow in one of Joseph's Spanish regiments, a Dutchman who, having served fourteen years in our 10th Hussars, was wounded in the Affair of Cavalry at Benaverte under Lord Paget, and had been taken at the hospital. Dine snugly, and drive away care—but with sobriety. Segovia three leagues from Otero.

Sunday, January 14, 1810.—Rise at half-past six. Breakfast. Start at eight. Weather very fine. Our unicorn answers perfectly. The worst of Segovia is the interior. Round the town there is an air of courtly antiquity, a curious wall with a tower, and an abrupt, rocky broken boldness of ground that renders the scene highly attractive. The antique towered wall, dilapidated by time, following the crest of a red precipitous rock, surmounted again by fretted towers and glittering spires that, with unequal loftiness, add variety to grandeur. This Coup d'Oeil prepares disappointment for the expecting traveller. The redness of the stone adds much to the warmth of the scene. Opposite the crest of the town rocks is another crest, and between the two runs a clear and plentiful stream, traversed by elegant bridges, and bordered by crowding trees and happy-looking cottages—they really were happy, till abominable war had hither stretched his iron hand! We soon come up with the convoy. 'Tis a corn country. The stream is a willowy stream, with sand-banks. Bare hills bound the view contiguous, strewed with good-looking villages. Mountains clad with snow are in the distant prospect. Over these hang flocks of cloud resembling birds. Road very bad. Pass a river by a bridge, and then through a pine-wood and divers villages, and arrive at half-past four at Sta. Maria de Meve, five leagues. Are met in the

square by an officer, who gives us our billet, which
is on the schoolmaster. We walk about the
village, which is considerable, but offers nothing
worthy of remark. We steer towards the Chef,
who gives us a wide berth. We repair to our
quarters, a snug little room, with a good pan
of fire. Beefsteaks, turkey, drumsticks grilled,
and potatoes getting ready below. We have
Muscadel, Madeira, and red Paxarate : so propose
to dine well. Good-night, my little red book : I
must talk to my companions.

Monday, January 15, 1810.—Rise at six.
Breakfast, and start prosperously. Weather fine,
dry and cold. In the prospect are very remarkable
heights not much above the horizon, cut off in the
prospective semicircle as with a scythe, and forming
an apparent table, without the slightest perceptible
deviation from the dead level. Road heavy sand
—very open—wine and corn country, clouded
with spacious woods and considerable villages, in
one of which I am now writing, and see from the
carriage windows women dressed with red gowns,
turned over their heads, displaying a bright yellow
petticoat, which is short enough to discover their
scarlet stockings. So that, grouped together to see
the convoy, they resemble a flock of huge birds
of gaudy plumage, running about one after the
other, and then stopping with undecided motion.
Road execrable. On the brow of a hill over-

hanging a stream stands a beautiful rich old castle, strikingly charming, well contrasted with a lean, high watch - tower. We ascend a terrific hill, then traverse large pine-woods. Shoot ahead of the convoy, and at seven o'clock arrive at Olmedo —six leagues, a considerable town. The French have taken here barricading precautions for their security. We get a good billet, and prepare as usual to be comfortable. The Table Mountains, which diversify this wide country, are very remarkable.

Tuesday, January 16, 1810.—Signora Nicolosa and her household are very unpleasant people. She puts on the courtesy of fear, but, finding us harmless, soon evinces her discontent and narrowness. At seven o'clock we start for Valdestilias. The river Eresma somewhat relieves the sameness of the country. The Chef comes up to the carriage and affects civility, telling us how admirably the English behaved to the French in Portugal. "Ay, ay" (swears), says he, "you are very snug (swears)—in a comfortable carriage (swears), although prisoners. Well—well—it ought to be so (swears); you behave to your prisoners magnificently (swears); I have good reason to say so (swears horribly). Had it not been for the exertions of Messieurs les Anglais, we should have been assassinated by hundreds—after the Convention." Dead bodies, half-devoured, are again seen. Arrive at

Valdestilias—deserted and destroyed! In searching about for some house that may not infect
or defile us (for here the convoy halts), we find
a venerable assembly, consisting of the clergy
of Salamanca, mounted on asses, led by the
venerable Dr. Curtis, whom I well remember,
supposed to be bound for France. Dr. Curtis is
a learned, respectable old man, who for thirty
years has been Rector of the Irish College at
Salamanca, which office is united to that of Rector
of the University, and now the French are drag-
ging him and his brother clergy, God knows
where or why! The French soldiers hoot them
as they pass. The doctor, however, preserves a
manly dignified spirit. Some little time ago the
Spaniards, under, I think, the Duque del Parque,
snatched Salamanca from the hands of their enemies.
But obliged again to retire, the French visit the
joy, and perhaps the aid, evinced by the clergy on
that occasion by this act of severity on their re-
entry. Our search for lodgment being fruitless,
we request of the Colonel that we may go on four
leagues more to Valladolid, which is granted. *Mais
soyez sages!* says the Chef. After baiting the
beasts, we set forward. Immediately below the
village a noble bridge leads us over the Eresma,
a smiling copious river. Road still sandy.
The swift part of our convoy and the one from
Salamanca have set forward, and are a mile ahead.

We wish to rejoin them on account of the patriot
banditti, which by daylight we do not fear, but
by night we do. The road dreadfully heavy sand
—slow—slow—slow ! Reach at length the *Douro*,
here a rapid, considerable, sea-green stream. " In
different and in distant places have I beheld thee,
fair stream," say I to myself ; "foaming under
the frown of rocky Toro, or swiftly laving the
vine-clad luxuriance that adorns thy track from
Lamego to Oporto." We have for some time
seen Valladolid away to the right, and to the left a
town with a castle on the site much resembling
Toro. Now we pass a half-eaten cadaver. This
bridge over the Douro is called the *Puente del
Douro*. It is · suspiciously barricaded, and the
village on the other side displays the terror
of the little garrison. Here we lose sight of the
convoy we did wish to reach. We are over-
taken by some Franco-Spanish grandee, escorted
by twenty-six cuirassiers, with brazen helmets, as
we are entering the awful pine-wood that stretches
between us and Valladolid. Night is falling.
The sand returns no sound as these fellows trot—
trot—trot away, leaving us ploughing the sand.
Their brazen casques, long, flowing, black horse-
hair plumes floating on their white cloaks, their
passing as if they saw us not, with steady onward
attention, and riding into the awful gloom which
overhangs the depths of the wood, and the still

silence which swallows the faint echoes of their
paces, altogether make the appearance spectral and
imposing.

The sand is so grievously heavy that Stephens
and Morgan are obliged to get out and walk all
the way.   And I, as I sit, inwardly revile the folly
that has thus a second time committed us by night
in the midst of these sanguinary scenes.   For seven
miles the heavy sand and deep wood continue,
and perfect darkness closes round us.

Very glad to get out of the wood !   Meet a
French officer on horseback with two soldiers, one
with and one without arms.   I let down the glass
and ask him how far it is to Valladolid.   "Mais,
mon dieu, monsieur," said he in great agitation.
" We have been lost in the fields these two hours—
have you never left the great road ? "—" No."—
" Thank God," exclaimed he, and the soldier
slammed his musket with great vehemence.   We
reach the suburbs of Valladolid.

From the gate the Sergeant of the guard sends a
soldier with us to the Commandant of the town, who
gives us what they call an invitation to the Municipality,—that is to say, " The Commandant de la
Place *invite la municipalité* to lodge," etc.   The head
of the Muncipality gives us a billet upon the English
College.   He calls me to the window to point out
the way, and says in an under voice, " I wish it were
possible for me to lodge you in a palace !   Indeed,

sir, the will (laying his hand on his breast and looking mournful) is not wanting!" The moon having risen, sets off the square to great advantage. The streets knee-deep in sludge. We are well received at the College by the Rector, Mr. Colborne, a mild honest man. He puts us into a comfortable room, and makes a blazing fire. We dine at ten o'clock. Go to bed at twelve, and fall fast asleep. Olmedo is six leagues from Valladolid.

Wednesday, January 17, 1810.—Finish breakfast by half-past one. The Rector invites us to dinner. I carry Marshal Mortier's letter to General Kellermann; not at home, leave it, go to the square. Though well sized, the houses are miserable and entirely deceived us last night. There is nothing in this huge town worth noting: nothing rises above mediocrity, and the much greater part of 8000 houses are old and wretched. The streets are flowing with mud, the squares heaped with filth, and the main sewers are open. Never such an assemblage of buildings offered so little attraction. Never so populous a city exhibited such marks of neglect and depopulation.

At five o'clock the Rector arrives, and tells us that the Salamanca clergy, having applied for their parole, had been offered it upon condition that they should be mutually responsible for one another; and that, on the failure of any one of them, twelve of their number should be shot! These hard conditions Dr. Curtis refused. We descend to dinner; much hospitality, and but little that we can eat. Of the three English collegiates at this College, one is a youth named Challenor who comes from Worksop. He has a large nose, but is otherwise agreeable.

Thursday, January 18, 1810.—At nine go to the Chef; he is not at home. We leave our names; receive the following invitation from General Kellermann :—

Printed.

Le Général de Division Kellermann prie M. le Capitaine Chas. Boothby de lui faire l'honneur de venir dîner chez lui. Aujourd'hui 18 Janvier à 5 heures.

R.S.V.P.

Yesterday the air was ice and promised snow, but to-day, though frosty, it is shiny and fine. Dine with Kellermann, who speaks English and is very gentleman-like and attentive. Gives me letters from Burgos, Vittoria, and Bayonne. Very good cookery, but bad wine. Kellermann talks of the Convention of Cintra and his trip to England. He laughs when he says that the English would not let him come to London; we wondering why they should not. He praises the Isle of Wight, where he was suffered to set foot on shore. He is in great distress for one of his aides-de-camp, whom the brigands have got hold of; and sent an English officer to propose

an exchange in vain. His English servant lights
me back to the College at night, and we talk by the
way. This man had fallen sick four miles (leagues,
I would say) from Corunna. He was in the 5th
Regiment during the retreat of Sir John Moore.
The Spaniards, he says, took their arms, loaded
them, and would have immediately killed them,
had it not been for the French. The Gallicans
even stripped to the skin the poor Englishwomen,
who sat fatigued or ill by the roadside. " General
Kellermann," says he, " is a fine man for everybody. But O Lord! sir, he behaved shocking
cruel to the Spaniards at *Alba di Tormes*. Ever
such a sight of 'em laid down their arms, fell on
their knees and cried, 'Prisoners! prisoners!' But
the General, the first man, rode in amongst them,
killing some with his pistol, then drawing his
sword and cutting and slashing with his own hand.
The Dragoons followed at a gallop, rode in amongst
them and cut them all to pieces. Their arms and
heads flew about! Oh! it was shocking!" He
also dwells with much horror on the behaviour of
the French to their Spanish prisoners. " Lord! "
says he, " when the poor devils be tired or sick
and can't come on, they'll take 'em behind a house
and put a couple of balls through 'em in a minute! "
This fact, which one fondly would hope incredible,
but which all the inhabitants have unceasingly
affirmed, is but too well corroborated by the

carcases of Spanish soldiers on the road, upon
whose bodies the uniform declares their nation, and
the wounds the manner of their death.

That the Spaniards, a people at once patriotic
and ferocious, should commit atrocious barbari-
ties on such invaders as the French, and that the
French should be disposed to retaliate amidst
the tumult of battle or the inebriation of conquest, cannot raise our wonder, though it fills us
with disgust. But we must see with amazement,
as well as horror, that the French soldiers have
attained that pitch of human butchery, which enables them to murder without emotion, amidst the
easy cheerful fellowship of a peaceable journey,
numbers of wretches, whose only crime is to be
sinking under disease, nakedness, hunger, and
fatigue. I may safely affirm that in the present
state of our army the officers would order such acts
in vain. The reason of policy alleged for these
monstrous massacres is, that if those wretches were
left sick on the road they would only serve to
strengthen the brigands. "But as for the English
soldiers," say the inhabitants, "they feed 'em and
treat 'em well!" The clergy of Salamanca are let
out of prison.

Friday, January 19, 1810.—We procure a
cart and two mules from the Chef, which make us
more simple arrangements. Start at nine; leave our
fire with regret. Before we go, I write to Captain

Walsh, General Belliard's aide-de-camp, and beg
General Kellermann to forward it, hoping that
through old Geils our safe arrival at Valladolid
may make its way to England. In starting, we
thank Mr. Colborne for much hospitality, whilst
deploring the hardships and contributions to which
the French subject them. He admits that, by
comparison with other religious houses, he has no
reason to complain.

The road is beautiful, the country open,
but at distance broken by mountains. Some
that approach the road have been anciently
occupied as military posts. The country has a
great appearance of richness, intersected by considerable rivers, traversed by handsome bridges.
The largest of these streams, which flows on our
left, is the Pisuerga, and waters extensive vineyards.
The weather is bright, but freezing intensely, with
a high wind. Luckily the road is so grand that
the carriage runs lightly, as our new mule is lamed
in the shoulder. At five o'clock arrive at Duenas,
six short leagues from Valladolid. It is a large place,
stationed like a ship in a rough sea, near the confluence of the Pisuerga and Carrion. Not liking
our first billet, get a second ; not liking that, ask the
woman servant of a large house next door if they
will take us in. "Non tenemos camas, señor"
(We have no beds, sir). "Las tenemos nos otros
Muchacha querida" (We have them ourselves,

dear wench). So she consents, but slips slyly over
to the next house to abuse the man who (she sup-
poses) has advised us to trouble her, and this mistake makes the street ring again. I have much
difficulty to still this storm, and then all goes well.
Intensely cold.

Saturday, January 20, 1810. — Freezing —
bright and clear—the road superb. The country
rich, open, beautified by a considerable frozen
river, superbly bridged, and broken by mountains.
Seven large glittering villages in sight at once.
On the roadside lies the body of a Spanish soldier,
with blood on his bosom. We are reconnoitred by
sixteen brigands on horseback, and being much in
rear of the convoy I wonder they did not attempt
us. At two o'clock we arrive at Torrequemada,
a large village half-burnt, sited on a hill overlook-
ing a twenty-three-arched bridge, which in a zig-
zag crosses the river Pisuerga, large and swift,
completely frozen and reflecting the sun—it adds a
brilliant gaiety to the scene. Torrequemada is four
fair leagues from Duenas, and here but for a meeting
convoy we should have halted. As it is, we proceed. Meet a large convoy and the 26th Regiment, almost all boys ; leave the great road and
steer four points from it to a village on the left. At
half-past five arrive at Herrera, six long leagues.
Lodge in a poor house, but pretty well for such a
poor village. The people, however, are very cordial ;

and our host tells exciting stories of brigands, and dwells with the greatest delight on the destruction of a detachment that was effected, three days gone, in this very village, an officer and thirty men. Says he : " Ay, that Valentian was a proper fellow. The officer came up joining his hands and crying, ' Prisoner ! prisoner !' but the Valentian plunged a sword into his breast, and it came out half a yard behind ! Ha ! ha ! ha !" This he repeats, and measures on his arm the length it came out. Mrs. Reynolds falls very ill. I get the good woman to put her to bed. A charming, pretty, elegant woman comes into the smoky kitchen, where I am sitting by the fire surrounded by Spaniards (Stephens and Morgan are upstairs). This be-witching woman, in her light blue gown, puts her laughing twinkling eyes into mine, and asks me what I say. "That you are very pretty," say I, although I had not spoken. "Mas guappo es Usted," returns she. "Pray tell me who you are?" I ask. "The surgeoness," she answers. "O! then you must go and see a poor English woman that lies sick."—"O yes, indeed," exclaims the hostess ; "the poor thing is very bad."—"But," rejoin I, "do you yourself profess chirurgical skill, or are you only the surgeon's wife ?" "Only the surgeon's wife," returns she, with a disclaiming shake of the head. "Then, pray, go and fetch your husband instantly !" Mine host now tells of a great battle in Valentia, and that Spaniards, English, and Portuguese made up 100,000 men. "Your authority, good mine host?"—"Our surgeon," says he, "went to shave the Commandant."—"Shave the Commandant!"—"Si senhor es Barbero tambien."—"Yes, sir, he's a barber also; and so the Commandant told him this news." (Enter Chirurgio-barber.) He greets us with ceremonious courtesy, and immediately asks for the lady. Hear our dialogue:—*Chi.* (pointing to me) "Is this her husband?" *Boo.* "You are come to prescribe for the woman. What have you to do with her husband?" *Chi.* (laughing heartily) "You say well! you say well! Ha! ha! ha! ha! Come along, then! come along! Where is the lady? But (stopping short), does she speak Castilian?" *Boo.* "Not a word!" *Chi.* (in despair) "Purest Virgin! how then shall I tell what ails her?" *Boo.* "Look at her and touch her." *Chi.* "Ay, that I can do!". *Boo.* "She has the headache, a stiff neck, and pains in her bones." *Chi.* (going out) "O! then we shall get on wondrously!" He soon returns, declaring she has a severe cold, for which he prescribes a dish of chocolate and a decoction of sauce flowers; both which being soon administered, the patient betters. Reynolds bears his wife's indisposition with wonderful fortitude. We dine very well; at dinner drink brandy-and-water, and crack a bottle of claret after. As we

go to bed, the floor gives great indications of a
capacity to lower us into the stable, it having
settled in the shape of a punch-bowl.

Sunday, January 21, 1810.—We are hurried
and bothered by a French officer, who is ordered
to wait with the rearguard to see us off, for it
seems these parts are full of brigands. " *Sacré
bleu,*" says the officer with rapid repetition ; while
sleepy Dilly, lazy Reynolds, and feeble Nelly Par,
walk over each other and dawdle into the harness
in such a lackadaisical manner that he naturally
loses all patience. When ready to start we offer
him a place in the carriage, which immediately
gives him back his good-humour, and he very
courteously declines our civility. We soon come
up with the rear of the convoy, which is at halt.
A musket goes off in front ! " It's finished," cries
a French soldier, laughing. Again !—two !—three !
four !—five !—six !—seven ! I let down the glass
and say to Stephens, who is walking, " What the
deuce is all that ? Are we in action with the
brigands ? "—" No ! " says he, with a black look,
" they're shooting Spanish prisoners ! " Again !—
eight !—nine ! " Holy God, pardon us ! " cries a
French soldier. " O, cursed Commandant ! " exclaims a French woman. We are penetrated with
horror, but hang on the hope that bullocks have
been the victims, not men. Moving on, however, we pass the lifeless bodies of two unhappy

wretches, who have thus required so many bullets
to despatch them. Close to the scene of action is
the murderous director. I look out of the opposite
window. Stephens looks at him without acknowledgment. Now he rides up to the window,
bowing and complimenting. Answer his questions
categorically. He says, "I have just been shooting two rascals! (swears). Thirty of the Spanish
prisoners have hid themselves in the wine-caves,
where the devil himself could not find them
(swears). I caught these two (swears), and have
made them an example to the rest (swears).
Thirty have got away (swears a great oath). It's
just so many brigands!"

This explanation, though far from satisfactory,
takes away the idea of wanton blood-spilling.
We look right on, gloomily grave, and he rides
off.

Although not entirely without excuse, this
act is clearly unjustifiable! If a prisoner runs
away, and the guard shoots him in the act, he
does no more than he ought, because when the
prisoner runs he is no longer surrendered, and
is an enemy, the capture of whom is doubtful.
But when he is retaken, you may put him in
irons, not to punish, but to secure him, for he
has committed no crime *and to kill him is murder*.

The carriage overturns in a ditch and wakes
Dilly. With the assistance of the French soldiers,

we are presently righted without damage.   At
half a league on our way we come to a little
shivering village, in which a party of French are
barricaded, and now enter again the great road,
which is superb.   Ascend the spur of a mountain,
and an interesting scene stretches below us.   A
wide plain bound in by broken mountains, which
are skirted by towered villages half-buried in
woods.   The Arlanza and Arlanzon, two copious
streams, intersect with majestic sweeps the fertile
plain, and make their confluence close to the road.
Their frozen currents, reflecting the gold sun,
streak the prospect as it were with flashes of
glorious diamond ; while the sun and frost and
snow light up the whole with magic touches.
Meet a battalion of the 1st Swiss and the 66th
with convoy.   Arrive at a poor village half-
destroyed, where a Captain, three subalterns, and
fifty Germans are barricaded.   We ask one of the
officers, a Dutchman, to eat bread and cheese.   He
declines, but entering into conversation expresses
himself after the following manner.

"Unhappy are we, condemned to serve in this
miserable country; above all, unhappy the Emperor's
foreign troops, who are invariably employed upon
every disagreeable and unprofitable duty!   On
our return to Madrid after the battle of Oceana,
nothing was heard of but the bravery and good
conduct of the *German troops*, and how much

they merited *reward*. *Behold our reward!* to be barricaded in this ruined village, surrounded by hordes of robbers, whose character excludes from one the consolation which, with other enemies, one might find in the hope of an honourable death! What is danger in the field of battle? If I die there, I die at once and die like a soldier. But to be taken by a band of barbarous, incensed thieves, who, after loading me with indignities, will torture me to death! What possible consolation can I find, impressed with the expectation of such an end? But three days ago, this village not being capable of sheltering a detachment, an officer and twenty - two men were sent on to *Herrera*. The brigands, fifty in number, entered the village, killed the officer and most of his men, taking the rest prisoners. This sort of thing happens every day, and may happen to me to-morrow! Every courier that arrives we are obliged to escort (for we have no Cavalry), and the danger is so great that no money could tempt me to take a turn for a comrade. You can have no idea of the number of men we lose. When our regiment entered this country, it was 3400 strong, and now we have but 600. We have been constantly in action, and lost 600 men at Talavera alone."

The officer having finished his complaint, I get into the carriage and wish him good-day. I

could not but hear him with more pleasure than
sympathy. As an individual, I wish him a better
plight; but as a part of Napoleon's horrid
instrument of wasting oppression, may dangers
and horrors complicate, multiply, and blacken
round him. Shall I not feel more, unhappy
Spain, for thy bleeding bosom and lacerated
heart! Land where, whatever the errors of
ignorance and superstition, the real God was
reverenced. The social hearth was decently
maintained, and the dues of hospitality and
honesty respected, and had in honour. Too
easily with all thy fire and intrepidity, too
quietly didst thou adhere to the love of order
and legal government. Thy King, though despicable as man, thou didst honour in his crown;
and by thy very loyalty wert thou betrayed.
Where, then, is the country whose sufferings shall
find a greater interest in my heart? My right
leg lies in thy fields. If it has served thee, thou
art welcome!

It appears from this German officer's complaint
that the predatory system of warfare adopted by
the Spaniards grows terrible and important. It is
no wonder that to prevent the increase of this
species of force the French should adopt cruel and
unjustifiable measures. At four leagues turn off
the road, and proceeding 500 yards arrive at Villa-
Topeque, a miserable, desolate collection of forty

poor houses. Pampliega, a considerable place, not half a mile off, sited on mid-mountain, would naturally have lodged us, but it is, they say, occupied by reinforcements from France. One officer tells 3000 Polish Lancers, and another 1500. The latter more probable.

We get a billet with the Spanish officers' prisoners, consisting of two Brigadier-Generals and three Colonels taken at Oceana. They joined our convoy from Valladolid in an old stage-coach drawn by four mules, which equipage General Kellermann, with a delicacy not much practised by either party towards the other, had provided in respect to their rank. They seem to be very agreeable, good-humoured old codgers. One of the Colonels belonged to Romana's army, Ildefonso Roxas. He was with Romana in the North, and was embarked by Admiral Keats at Nyebourg. He wears a sort of pendant star given by the King of England, inscribed *La Patria es mi Norte*. On his arm is embroidered in two places, *Se distingue en Medelin*. He was brought to King Joseph at Oceana, who offered to make him a General if he would serve him; but O'Farrel interposing observed that he was from the North. Upon which the King in a rage told him he should be shot. But O'Farrel, interceding, begged the King to spare his life, which His Majesty mercifully accorded, but reproached him with

deserting France and loving the English. "Sir,"
replied the Spaniard, "Spain has made peace with
England, and so have I."—"Take him away,"
cried the offended monarch.

I have great difficulty in getting upstairs, but,
animated by the excessive cold, I overcome all
obstacles; have much greater difficulty in getting
down, but, rendered desperate by the dread of
suffocation from the smoke, I succeed, and issue
from the house, weeping with smarting eyes, and
panting with the laboured respiration of resuscita-
tion. The Spanish grandees get another house.
While Stephens and Morgan endeavour to ameliorate
our tenement, I stroll to a huge bonfire, which the
soldiers have made in the little *Place* of the village.
Here I warm, and there comes to me the poor
French officer who would fain have had the fourth
place in our vehicle. He talks English with deliberate confidence. "How do you do, my dear?"
"Ah! for me I go from bad to worse. One of my
legs is quite—quite—*forlorn!*"—"Ha! ha! ha!
poor fellow! forlorn—ha! ha! ha!" says Morgan,
as he comes to fetch me to our cabin. It is a little
dark cave with black beams. Notwithstanding, we
eat the back of a roast turkey broiled, a good
mutton-chop, and hot potatoes, moistening the
repast with our remaining brandy and two bottles
of claret. When I would turn into the hole in
which my bed is crammed it is too short, but I

prefer lying crooked to defiling my bed by a contact with the floor, which is like a hardened dunghill.

Monday, January 22, 1810.—Rise at half-past five ; breakfast in peace—ready in time ! Morning intensely cold and threatens snow. The mighty coach of our Spanish friends leads off, and we follow. One of them, Colonel Ramon Salvador, is a wondrous, dirty, blackguard-looking little fellow, and talks exquisite English very fast ; swearing tremendously, with a laughing face. These good Spaniards take me for a General, and call me *el General Ingles*, and say " buenas dias el Senhor General." This tickles me so much, that I have not yet found in my heart to undeceive them. We enter the magnificent great road. It begins to snow like blazes. In the midst of it we meet the Polish Lancers, fine savage - looking dogs ! They seem to wag their whiskers in the snow. The flags to their lances give them a very striking appearance. Other Cavalry are with them amounting to about 1000. 2000 Infantry also are with them belonging to Loison's Division coming from Vittoria ; so that it appears no reinforcements, at least of Infantry, have reached thus far. The snow ceases after an hour's feathering and it becomes fine. View, streams of willows like the Fens of Lincolnshire ; road charming, moderate mountains, corn and wine. Celada di Camino, two leagues, a better sort of village ; pass other villages, too, by the same sort of road.   Evening falls, and we discover the towers and spires of Burgos.   For the last three leagues the road has passed through an avenue of stately trees, and the entry into Burgos is thickly wooded by them.   At seven o'clock arrive at Burgos ; snowing again.   Get out of the carriage and walk to the Municipality.   They see at once we are English ; talk a good deal of patriotism, and give us a wretched billet up two hundred stairs.   Disagreeable people with much palaver ; a filthy room, stinking like an Augean stable !   I find poor Mrs. Reynolds almost senseless in the kitchen, and not one of the inhuman women offering her the least assistance.   I reproach them, and a man who sits profoundly idle in the chimney-corner proves to be a physician.   Ask his advice. The tinker Colonel enters and disputes with him, maintaining cathartic against emetic.   I assist the physician, and drive the Colonel from the field, who makes submission, does Ramon Salvador. Eat with appetite ; but palpable stink mixes with our food.

Tuesday, January 23, 1810.—Excellent butter by way of rarity.   Wait on General Solignac with the letter General Kellermann had given me.   Wait an hour and a half, the premier aide-de-camp insisting on my stay.   Said aide-de-camp a remarkably mild gentleman-like man who, as well as his General, served in Portugal with Junot ; speaks well of

Admiral Cotton. The General at length descends
in a dirty greatcoat, woollen stockings about his
heels, unshaved, his manners not prepossessing.
Refuse to breakfast with him à la fourchette, but
accept his invitation to dinner. Go with Stephens
and Morgan to see the cathedral, which is eminently
beautiful—a great assemblage of fretted, shelly
spires seen from every point. In the middle a
tower, not enough mounted. Next we go shop-
ping; weather inclined to snow, cold and raw. A
Franco-German surgeon is very attentive to Mrs.
Reynolds. Repair to dine with General Solignac.
A noble fire irradiates the room. The General's
manners are very pleasing on proof. His enuncia-
tion, slow and deliberate, gives a pleasing novelty to
the French tongue; his conversation pointed and entertaining. He has no use of his left hand, which
is covered by a glove. He had a shot through it
at the battle of Vimiera. He thinks that had he
been taken prisoner the English surgeons would
have cut it off; complains that they are addicted
to excessive amputation, and had an idea they were
specially paid for it. At dinner sit next to the
Chef, who makes the capable. The General dis-
courses much of his gambling adventures in
different parts of the world. At Milan a famous
charlatane cheated him, " Je me jettais sur lui
comme un coup de foudre. ' Robber ! ' said I,
' restore me the money you have stolen '—ce qu'il

16

me faisait de suite!"—that sort of man. After dinner the crowd disperses, and the General asks me amongst a few others to go upstairs to coffee. Upstairs we find a luminous, vigorous fire. The General puts me in an armchair and extends himself in another, and lets the rest provide for themselves. He speaks with the most lively indignation of the financial chicanery of Joseph's Government. "I have staked my cent mille francs on the stability of their Government," says he; "had it been overthrown, my cent mille francs went with it. But now that I would not scruple to place my fortune—the inheritance of my son—at the foot of Gibraltar, what pretence in the world have they for giving me their paper at a depreciation of two-thirds? It's robbery, gross robbery, and no other thing. I give you my word of honour [lays his hand on his breast], I give you my solemn word of honour, that the very next public money that comes this way I will stop and pay myself my cent mille francs! nets! C'est ce que je ferai, ou diable m'emporte, bien sur! précisément ça! allez!" The French officers stand aghast, which provokes the General to renew his asseveration with additional solemnity. He asks me to dine again to-morrow, which I decline on account of my companions. Find Stephens and Morgan asleep in the persuasion that we march to-morrow. Have what the French term a *nuit blanche*.

Wednesday, January 24, 1810.—Morgan wakes us at four o'clock and wonders we don't get up, till, having awakened Stephens three times, who would fain sleep, he is obliged in his own defence to tell him we do not march. We stroll about the town, which is very good. The gateway bears a full-length basso-relievo of Charles V. The river looks stylish and commercial, and the row of fine houses along its right bank resembles the Marinas of the Mediterranean. Though less than Valladolid, it is ten times, nay, twenty times, better. Write to the Colonel to relieve our baggage-cart. He begins "My dear Captain," and gives an evasive answer. Write to the General, who instantly complies. Beg him to forward to Madrid a letter for Geils. There is here a very elevated and pre-eminent citadel, in the fortifications of which recent pairs are visible. On that eminence the cathedral should have been built. Mercy on us, how grand it had been! As it is, it is much obscured.

Thursday, January 25, 1810.—Mrs. Reynolds worse. Write to the Chef to beg he will put her in some covered conveyance ; he gives no answer. Make up as well as we can with our beds. Weather improved ; snows now and then. Road still superb through an avenue of trees ; corn country. Meet about 1000 Cavalry, ill-mounted, of the 10th, 22nd, and 26th Regiments. At four leagues is the village

of Monasterio, where a group of men, women, and
children, standing on a bank that overhangs the
roads, throw quantities of huge biscuits to their
unhappy countrymen.   'Tis a very moving sight.
The country, the prospect, the road, the culture,
the soil visibly improving as we get on ; the road,
straight as a dart, loses the sight amidst the border-
ing trees.   At nightfall turn off a little to the left
and proceed to Vriviesca, a considerable town.
Are lodged at the house of the Padre Cura, a
Spaniard! a Schedoni in figure.   Comfortable
house, good people.   This town famous for valour
and true principles.   Send for the physician to
Mrs. Reynolds.   On account of his general talents
and sagacity, he goes by the name of *Mrs. Pitt.*
'Tis a little humpy, crook-legged, hook-nosed,
sharp, funny-looking mortal.   Wen on forehead,
cocked hat, square to the front ; has been prisoner
in Ireland, never so happy in his life.   The
Captinis and Milordes took him to coffee-houses
and gave him *iggs, melk, bride, botto* (all pro-
nounced with the most laboured articulation) ; and
then took him home to dinner, where they made
him drunk with punch and put him to bed.
"O !" he exclaims, "what fine times !   When I
had dressed myself in the morning my work
was done for day !" (a type of the Spanish idleness).   Mrs. Reynolds may travel without danger,
and is not very bad.   He refuses his fee, saying

that he had a fever in Ireland, and that the faculty would not take anything from him, but gave him many shelligs and pekkies. A short time ago he was summoned to Burgos and charged with animating the brigands,—a mighty, droll, honest little fellow! Several valiant women come to see us. One, a fruit-seller, had, with her fist, knocked down three Frenchmen in the market-place in presence of *Murat*, who applauded her. As an instance of the incredulity of the Spaniards to the reports of the French, the curate tells us that Buonaparte was at Madrid some time before the Priviescars were convinced that he had passed through their town! They are in a greater degree credulous on the other side of the question. That 200,000 *Moorish cavalry* had come over from Barbary to their assistance was perhaps not the most incredible thing firmly believed by all ranks of Madrid. The Padre Cura sleeps in the same room with us, and snores all night like a bassoon.

Friday, January 26, 1810.—Pass the convoy before daylight and join the coaches ; road elegant ; rains pretty heavily. Go off at a round trot, which lasts until four leagues from Vriviesca. We approach the romantic scenery of Pancorvo, where a rock like Gibraltar traverses the way. How we can pass it we know not. For colours, boldness of outline, harmony and keeping, this rock surpasses any that I have seen. The road wriggles through it with majestic breadth, great design, and beautiful contrivance, sloping with gentleness, now cut through the rock, and now built over the dell. The rocks, with a natural scarp of 300 feet plumb down upon the road, form for half a mile a continued pass, never to be forced, and as little to be turned. I would trust the security of my kingdom on its strength, if occupied with judgment. Issuing from this defile, which looks like the den of a giant, we stretch our eyes over a beautiful and very changed country, and the road, forming a noble avenue as straight as a dart for many miles, stretches through a luxuriant tract, finely varied with mountains, woods, and villages, laughing amidst the fertility of a rich black soil. Arrive in very good time and some hours before the convoy at Miranda del Ebro, a little tiled town. Pass the Ebro by a pretty light bridge to get to the Commandant of the Place, as the river severs the town in twain. Get a billet upon the apothecary, who shows us into a large and perfectly naked room, whence I could drop an egg into the Ebro, which is here a struggling stream, sundered by islands, maybe seventy yards across ; bottom shelvy rock, probably fordable in many parts hereabouts ; banks open soil, current not rapid. Miranda is twenty leagues from its source. The weather is very mild. The cursed woman refuses to admit Mrs. Reynolds on account of her illness, and in the

midst of the abuse we bestow on each other
Stephens announces the elopement of the muleteer
with his car and mules. I brush off to the Commandant over the bridge again, and hasten into the
levee-room. A French officer, proud to display
his acquirements, comes up and says in a quick,
offhand style, "*What do you believe?*" I have
the good fortune not to let my countenance go,
but answer gravely in French, as if he had said
"*What do you want?*" in the best English in the
world. His reputation in languages thus confirmed to the admiring auditors, he orders us
another car with the greatest alacrity. Repass the
Ebro; return to the naked room, now cheered by
some crackling faggots. Mrs. Reynolds is better
lodged in a less inhospitable dwelling. Stephens
superintends the mutton-chops, Morgan the potatoes, whilst I, more ambitious, undertake an omelet
and the melted butter; these with the redundant
addition of pork chops, and enlivened by two
bottles of pure claret,—what should we do but lay
aside our cares with our greatcoats, and refresh
ourselves merrily?

Saturday, January 27, 1810.—Mrs. Reynolds
much better yesterday and to-day. Our cart to-
day is a leetle wee carty, with two leetle wee
bullocks. Set forward at daylight; road bad,
heavy and hilly. A German, deserted from the
French and become an officer of brigands, hangs

on a bran-new post by the roadside. In front of us a curious church forms the pinnacle of a high mountain. A pretty river of verdigris forms graceful cascades of green silk with white fringe. Pass the confine of Old Castile and enter Alava, of which Vittoria is the capital; but before we reach the green river see on a rock close to the road a frozen waterfall, which has a most beautiful and surprising appearance. Traverse an irrigated plain. The soil black. In the boundary of the prospect plenty of gay villages, goodly towered, picturally coloured, in clusters of trees, at the foot of wooded or castle-topped mountains. Road still an avenue, but heavy with sludge ; weather not sunny, but serene and freshly soft. Halt to refresh at Puebla de Arraganzan, a miserably dirty and resourceless town. Morgan eats a quantity of garlic in the shape of a sausage ; Stephens and myself divide a black pudding, which, by way of guarantee, the filthiest hag we ever saw assures us she made with *her own hands — such* hands ! On leaving this place enter into enchanting scenery, where the beautiful green river bottoms in large basins and busy cascades. The richly-clothed, broken and fantastic mountains impend over the road with awful grandeur ; on the shaggy top of one of these is an old mouldering turret. This romantic scene soon changes for one but little remarkable. At dusk arrive

at Vittoria, five long leagues from Miranda. It
is situated advantageously on an eminence, has
the appearance of a fine town, which it supports
on proof. The square is not very large, but perfectly uniform, noble, and finished. The French
never lost their hold of this town, which therefore
has never been subjected to those rude vicissitudes
which have spoiled the other Spanish cities. No
very gorgeous building insists upon instant notice ;
but the liberality of the houses generally, the
breadth and perfect pavement of the streets, give
it a metropolitan air unmixed with meanness, seldom observable even in the very first-rate towns
of Spain. Vittoria was a very rich trading city,
giving chiefly iron in exchange for the commodities
of England and France. The former branch of
her trade the unceasing protection of France has,
of course, strangled. And in respect to the
latter she is not left in very advantageous circumstances, from the contributionary system under
which she labours, and the embarrassment which
the incessant transit of the military machines
throws upon land carriage. Dark, dark, before we
get lodged in the house of a physician, a comfortable house, but cold reception, except from his
daughters, who seem very glad to see us. The
second is very pretty, but fourteen years old,
graceful hair and laughing eyes, very good-
humoured and agreeable.

Sunday, January 28, 1810.—We bustle up betimes, long ere the day breaks, and despatch Dilly to the Forum to procure a baggage-cart from him who distributes the means of transport. The Chef keeps poor Dilly till every soldier's servant is provided for and the whole convoy in motion ; and at last, on going myself into the square, I am fortunate enough to get a slow bullock-cart, and not till eight o'clock we start in rear of everything. *So* disagreeable ! road execrable ! Country fully peopled, and cultivated. Serene soft weather. Though of fine frame, the road is hideous for want of repair, in great holes, etc. Being in rear of the shrieking, creaking, cree-cree carts, added to the sudden change in the road, ruffles the surface of our minds, and prevents our enjoying the fineness of the weather or the prettiness of the scenery. Our only hope is to be able to shoot ahead when the convoy halts. It halts at a village two leagues from Vittoria, in such a way that we find ourselves stuck on a narrow bridge where, *ne* backwards, *ne* forwards, *ne* on one side—no, no ! here we are fast enough ! Get out and walk, to my knee in sludge, through the town, and get on a bank a quarter of a mile on. Here will I wait for the vehicle. My spirit plumes herself and looks abroad, uninterrupted and no longer deafened with the noise, nor shaken by the long prospect of the slow-trailing convoy. Some boy-regiments pass upwards, and are bantered

en passant by the old blood-spillers going down—
106-120—not Frenchmen. There is a sleepy,
half-sulky carelessness about Dilly that moves me
from the little moderation I possess. Forever he
leaves the horses by themselves on the sides of
precipices where the difference of a hair would
dash us to atoms. Am more fidgety than a woman,
and swear like a trooper. Without having made
any very remarkable ascent, lo! a wonderful scene
suddenly opens on our view. Looking out of
the right-hand window, the eye falls 10,000
fathoms down and gazes with rapture on the
luxuriant and indescribable beauties of Nature,
admirably mingled with the works and dwellings of
men, scattered with the most lavish and fantastic
variety. Plumb down! as if soaring with the
wings of yon eagle that animates the scene, we gaze
with insatiate pleasure and ever-growing admiration
at the luxuriant abundance and vivid colouring
of vegetation; and as the swain gazes on the
face of his beloved, contemplating separately and
at once the fascinating beauty of her features, so
our eyes dwell with rapture on those wild, graceful,
ever-changing forms which the wonder-working
waters have impressed upon the earth, and which
now lie spread before us in countless variety, clothed
in all the splendid, glowing, but ever chaste colouring of Nature. As the road obtains upon the
rugged steep on whose side it is formed, more and

more wonderful features rise up in prospect and snatch us from the preceding objects of admiration. The vast but softly-moulded mountains in the foreground, richly clothed with woods, with verdure, and with rushing waters, shoot towards each other their mossy slopes with hasty swiftness or majestic deliberation, while herds and flocks ramble over their awful steeps with native familiarity. Underneath, the splendid vales, or rather mighty ravines, are adorned by cascading rivers, that with a beautiful inconstancy wind amongst the villages, orchards, and gardens which everywhere emboss this luxuriant land. Numerous bridges overspan the trembling streams, contrived with a rudeness whose simplicity is elegance, and some so overgrown with ivy as that they seem but arching bowers for the light tread of aerial beings. White gulls floating over the dark ground seem flashes of light. Over the aspiring tops of these amazing high mountains in foreground, still higher and horrid uplift their dun, sleet-covered heads, boldly tracing in the horizon, with a rocky line, overhanging steeps and highly-pointing spires. The road, in majestic breadth descending the steep side of the mountain, takes us to Nasconaza, a comfortable village three leagues off—it is a league farther to Escoriessa, a good town. The people know and salute us. Again half a league to Achavaleza, a good town. Scenery still kept up. About dark descend to Mondragon, five long leagues of excessive bad road, but soft weather all day. We are billeted at the house of a good old woman, who looks to be at least four hundred years old ; she does not know how old she is now, but knows that in six years she shall be fourscore. Am surprised at my own ignorance that the language of Biscay, called by the speakers of it Basco or Bascuenza, is not more Spanish than Welsh or Erse is English. Those who have not studied Spanish do not understand one word spoken by a Castilian. An interesting, funny little girl is of the greatest use to us ; she makes herself understood in very odd French, and busies herself mightily for us, reproaching the people, astounding the dull, and then laughing at their astonishment, throwing herself into all the energetic attitudes of impatience. Reynolds in walking across the street from the carriage to the house loses his master's case, containing a couvert of silver. This troubles Stephens exceedingly. How the devil *he could lose it* in that little space !

Monday, January 29, 1810.—Have great difficulty in getting a cart for our baggage, but with the help of my little girl *Bustle* I get one. The Chef, in a fury because the carts escape, gives most savagely the *coup plat de sabre* to the first wretch that meets him. A sweet pretty Biscayenna comes into the room and asks if we have lost anything,

at the very instant that Stephens is offering a
reward to *Bustle* if she will find *his couvert*. The
Biscayenna found it in the street, and says she
does not choose to profit by any accident at the
expense of a stranger and an Englishman. Pretty
Biscayenna, the reward you obtain thus honestly
will give you more pleasure than the most costly
findings !

More than any other part of Spain that I have
seen by a great many degrees, is the Province of
Biscay flourishing and populous. The most
avaricious and precise cultivation, added to the
irrigated fertility of the soil, ensures a luxuriant
produce. The tillage extends to the very tops of
the highest mountains where there is soil, and this
Province supplies all the neighbouring ones with
butter and cheese. The cattle are very small and
nicely proportioned. Beef and mutton both very
good. But the disproportioned population and
industry of this part of Spain is attributed to
another cause besides the natural advantages of
the terrene, and that is the state of liberty which,
until lately, its inhabitants had been happy enough
to preserve ; for they maintained extraordinary and
essential privileges, which put them far above any
part of the Peninsula subjected to the Crown of
Spain. They paid no duties whatever to the King,
being taxable only by their particular juntas, to
which His Catholic Majesty applied occasionally

for pecuniary assistance, which was granted or denied as the junta thought fit. Biscay was equally exempt from any tribute of soldiers, nor could any troops be quartered on the people except by permission of their Provincial Government. If a Biscayan, say they, committed a capital crime in any other province, or even in the metropolis, capital punishment could not be inflicted unless the criminal was sent to be judged in his own Province.

Thus these people, allowed the advantages of their soil and mercantile situation, are industrious, and by consequence rich. In other countries equally fertile, as in Sicily for instance, rich land lies neglected, because tyranny, stupidly greedy, lays on taxation with an ignorant hand, and mars the prosperity of the land-owner. The Biscayans are the most sensible, cleanly, civilised, and amiable class of Spaniards I have seen, and not only from patriotism dislike the French, but because King Jo is equalising them with the rest of his subjects. Start at nine o'clock alone. It begins to rain, soon ceases, and now is beautifully soft and fresh. Road rather better. Meet, in separate battalions, 1800 Cuirassiers, fine men, well mounted and appointed. The officers' helmets richly gilt and ornated with silver. From the crest descends, glossy and with free silky fluency, the copious horse-hair. We come to a village, and turning a corner come upon the convoy at halt. This is about half-journey, where the great road to Bilbao turns off on the left. About 7000 Infantry file by us here; very many boys. An officer of the Irish Legion accosts us, and walks with us a good way—a fine active young fellow — and exerts himself much to prevent plunder. I take him to be a West Indian. 36,000 men, he says, have been embarked at Portsmouth for Spain—doubt not! He presses us to stop at some wine-house and drink at his expense. This we disincline, and therefore decline to do. Leaving this village, which is considerable, we wind steeply to an immense height; leaving an enchanting scene behind us, laughing to be cheered in January by the beams of the illustrious sun, wind down the mountain, and open upon scenery less inviting. A spiral mountain is remarkable ahead. At half-past three arrive at Villareal, a small town. We are billeted in the same house with our friends the Spanish Generals, and in our room is a fine fire. Hear various political reports from a rich and obliging Biscayan — Archduke Charles declared Emperor, renewal of the Austrian war, and so forth; don't believe one word! Four leagues we have come to-day.

Tuesday, January 30, 1810. — Start at eight. File in rear of the coaches; meet 2000 horse-hair Cavalry, and 9000 Infantry of a better description

than yesterday, newly equipped.   They pelt Nelly
Par with turnips.   We arrive at Villafranca, two
and a half leagues ; enter the château of a marquis,
from the back of which we have a most enchanting
view of the spiral mountain, from which the French
country lies open to the eye.   Admirable gardens,
orchards, rivers, woods, and green fields—a paradise ! a paradise !

This mountain is in a range which branches
from the Pyrenees and runs in a direction parallel
to the coast of Biscay at about thirty miles' distance from it.   It was this range we passed when
the scenery delighted us so about Mondragon, and,
having traversed it, we now behold it on the right
hand and on the starboard bow.   Villafranca, a
very good but small town ; walking out of it
and looking back, I see it in a beautiful posture
backed by fertile mountains.   A lovely Biscayan,
whose open smile is like the sunshine, and who
steps over the earth as if it were no bar to her
progress, accompanies the convoy as it approaches
Tolosa.   Old Brigadier Domingo is instantly cap-
tivated, but she rejects his suit with frankness and
good-nature, unaccompanied by the slightest embarrassment.   At dusk we bring in sight Tolosa, with
milk-white houses, under circumstances of the most
enchanting beauty—in a bottom enveloped by rich
and fantastic mountains and watered by the river
Oriia.   Tolosa is a good, populous town.   We

17

are sent to the Inn with the Spanish brigadieros—
a very good house. This day's journey has been
five long leagues through the most glowing and
romantically-beautiful country I ever saw, all the
way winding through the vales, whereof there is
none that does not speak prosperity and abundance
—shining single houses, gardens, orchards, large
villages, strew the land as thick as hail. And the
most rigid cultivation clothes it with inconceivable
splendour. The day has been heavenly, and the
beams of the sun, piercing the mist of the mountains, sparkled in the frequent cascades which the
charmed eye was ever catching through the leaf-
less woods or auburn foliage. Some of the horse-
hair Cavalry tarry here to-night. Tolosa five long
leagues from Villareal—ay, long ones!

Wednesday, January 31, 1810.—Start at eight
o'clock, meet 2000 horse-hair Cavalry—a heavy-
shouldered, labouring horse hard worked. The
officers' helmets seem solid gold, gorgeously em-
bossed ; the most graceful and complete warrior's
head-dress I ever saw. The men uncommonly
fine. Meet a troop of Horse Artillery—four
6-pounders, two $5\frac{1}{2}$-howitzers, twenty tumbrels,
sixty caissons or thereabouts. Meet 5000 Infantry
—grown, but not fine men—newly equipped.
Charming weather. Road, mending apace, goes by
the side of the river Oriia, which, receiving the Elzain
at the good village of Andoarn, becomes a fine-

looking river, and one would think in some degree
navigable.   It empties itself into the Bay of Biscay
about two leagues west of St. Sebastian.   Andoarn is
two leagues from Tolosa.   At Unheta, two and three
quarter leagues, a small but good village (good, for
all the houses are town houses ; no such thing as a
cottage), the road resumes its excellence.   Country
beautiful, but less exquisite than elsewhere.   The air
is cooler than yesterday.   At ten o'clock the sun
appeared in splendour.   It is not twelve, and Hernani peeps above a steep hill most attractively, a
quarter of a mile off, backed by noble mountains that
reach the clouds and glory in the sun.   See a child
drawing a vegetable-cart, the body the shell of a
gourd, and the wheels two flat turnips.

Arrive at Hernani at quarter-past twelve, a nice
little town, three leagues.   Take *café au lait* at a
dirty French coffee-house.   The scene behind this
house, glistening in the sun, with a river running
past, is superb.   Start at one o'clock in pre-
cedence of the convoy.   Scenery on leaving the
town, Elysium !   Where are the terms of sufficient praise ?   I am forced perpetually to use the
same, yet are the scenes the same ?   O no !
ever varying, ever changing, yet ever lovely !
Submit, dull mortal, to your trammels, and describe
things as you may.   What a sweet trout river !
How *populous* the country is !   Have I mentioned
before that the Biscayan women universally have

enormous flat queues that descend considerably below the waist? In some of the towns two queues hang from the back of the head straight down, or sometimes tucked under the zone.

The men dress in all sorts of gaudy colours and flowered jackets, flannel leggings stripped black and white, and red sashes. Before we came to Hernani we met what the Austrian bulletins termed an armour-equipped cavalier—a cuirassier. His whole body and head was in steel, which looked beautiful, and must be a marvellous protection. Raven horse-hair flowed glossy down his casque abundant. The scenery is always in bursts of laughter. Away on the pinnacle of a mountain to the right a huge obelisk points upwards. Mountains in front broken and grand; road hilly. Meet Artillery—ten 9-pounders, four 8-inch howitzers, seventy-three tumbrels, four of which are saddled and slung for men to ride on, eight spare carriages, sixteen open waggons, five caissons, three forge carts. Now Infantry; 6000 fine lads, newly equipped. In ascending the hill to Ollarsu, met seventy-eight covered waggons or caissons, and two with Engineers' stores. All the Artillery and equipage we meet is new. Ollarsu is a small good town, five leagues from Tolosa. The coaches, which we join here, set off before us. They are better horsed than we, and soon leave us. It grows dusk, and we have a long hilly

league to Irun. Our friends the Spanish brigadiers
call a council of war. We declare our intention
to proceed ; they fear to go without the convoy.
Con dios, ustedes! Meet a French officer.
" Messieurs," says he, " this road is much infested
with brigands, and you risk yourselves much, being
so few in number. At this time of evening especially no distinctions of nation will avail. I met
about quarter of a league on a number of carriages,
which I recommend you by all means to join.
You will soon do it if you push on. It is but a
few minutes since I myself was fired at." Merci,
monsieur, merci bien! We disbelieve monsieur
and proceed. Very heavy hills and deep woods.
It gets dark. A shot fired behind us! Begin to
believe monsieur! *Another shot!* Diable! I hope
they'll hail the carriage before they fire at it! Ho!
ho! here we are! Irun! It is not yet seven o'clock.

Seek the Commandant de la Place ; find at his
house our Chef. He takes his leave of us desiring
us to present ourselves to the Commandant de la
Place à Bayonne—glad to have done with him.
After providing ourselves, etc., meet one of the
Spanish brigadieros on horseback. They had
spoken to the same officer who told us he had
been fired at, and soon after, hearing the shots we
also heard, they thought it prudent to go back to
Ollarsu, where meeting the Chef he desired them
to come on, and here they are at nine o'clock, sorry

they did not follow our example. Take leave of these Spaniards. These were they—(1st) Brigadier-General Domingo Lasala, Colonel of the African regiment which at Talavera behaved so well, sharp shooting on the right of the British, where he was himself severely wounded in the arm. A good, honest, loyal, brave, jolly, comely old fat Spaniard! (2nd) Brigadier-General Marmillotti, a mild, thin, squeaking, tall, pale, genteel old woman! (3rd) Lieutenant-Colonel Jose Rivas, Colonel of Cavalry of the North, a stout-hearted, loyal, cut-and-thrust hussar, covered with wounds and medals; believes all good news! I pleased him greatly by giving him the king's arms in silver fretwork which I took from Towers's gorget. (4th) Colonel Ildefonso Roseas, captain of a frigate, a good-looking gentleman, quiet and good-humoured. (5th and last) Lieutenant-Colonel Ramon Salvador, surnamed the tinker, a little, queer-built, punch-faced, olive-coloured, laughing, dirty, smutched-artificer-looking, honest, friendly, intelligent, up-to-snuff Timothy. He speaks in English which cannot be understood.

What I have commonly comprehended under the name of Biscay contains three provinces which have nothing in common, but have laws, customs, and languages totally distinct. The first which joins Castile is Alava, of which Vittoria is the capital; next Biscaya, of which Bilbao is the capital;

and then Guipuscoa, of which St. Sebastian is the capital. Seven leagues to-day. We are lodged in a schoolroom and sleep on the copy-books.

Thursday, February 1, 1810. — Start at ten o'clock A.M. ; a nasty little uninviting town, this Irun, marshy and cold going out. At one mile arrive at the river Bidasoa, which here divides Spain and France. The wooden bridge which crosses it is occupied by the transit of 5000 Infantry. These dogs jeer as they pass us. Now the wooden bridge is clear ; on this side is a Custom-House lodge. The officers make some demonstration of searching our baggage, which being understood as a hint for some silver, we pass the bridge without further let and enter France !

The frontiers of the two countries have nothing remarkable on either side, but are strikingly un-amiable contrasted with the gorgeous beauties of Guipuscoa. But as we penetrate, a striking and general difference from Spain obtains. The scenery and enclosures are of great beauty and have a very English aspect. The style of cultivation, too, is English. The snow - clad Pyrenees mount the sky on the right ; on the left the sea— the sea, our proper domain—breaks upon our view through a heavy mist. It will be difficult for those who have never seen it under similar circumstances to conceive the fondness and softened recollections with which we gaze upon it. It holds us long in silence. Its waves, noiseless from the distance, flow gently to the land, and seem to welcome us and offer us liberty and protection, and tell us they surround our darling island, and keep from her the calamities and horrors we have witnessed. *May they ever!* May England's happiness and high favour continue long after we have ceased to breathe! The road is very fine, continuing over the tops of the hills. At two leagues arrive at Ouronne, the first French town, a small place; the people speak a miserable patois unintelligible to a Frenchman. We catch a glimpse of the sea now and then, and we could throw a stone into the last dip. Arrive at St. Jean de Luz, a considerable seaport town, pier, harbour; two rivers enter the sea here. The view up the river is enchanting; leave the sea somewhat and arrive at Bayonne, six leagues at half-past six.

CHAPTER XXIV

MY DEAR MULCASTER,—I send this letter *via* England,
and hope it will reach you. Having lost all hope of exchange in Spain, and conceiving strong hopes of effecting
it in France from my being disabled, and assisted by the
influence of Marshal Mortier, I at last determined to
undertake the journey, particularly as in France, if I were
obliged to live there for some time, my life would pass
more agreeably, I should hear more of what was going
on in the world, feel altogether nearer home, and get rid
of the horrors incident to feeling myself in the midst of
a vast uncivilised dispirited country. I bought a comfortable light post-chaise at Madrid, and two other officers,
my friends, promised a pair of beasts, that is to say, a
mare and a mare mule. The roads being unsafe, we
were obliged to travel with a convoy escorted by Infantry
—some of our halts were in miserable villages. We were
obliged to carry everything with us, beds and provisions,
etc., although creeping after bullock-carts for twenty-five
days. The distance of about 400 miles was tedious and
very disagreeable, added to the bad lodgings and the
constraint of a convoy ; yet, upon consideration, sitting
all day in a comfortable carriage, and sure of cover,
victuals, and a bed at night, with two agreeable com-

panions,' being well recommended to the Generals in the cities, who were ready to lend occasional assistance, although I look back with great satisfaction on this Spanish journey as a thing over, I cannot boast to have endured any of the real evils of life. On the contrary, comparing experience with expectation, I find myself obliged to congratulate myself on my good fortune. Travelling in the depth of winter, we only found a little severity about Burgos, before it was fine, and afterwards up to this day it has been heavenly. One of my companions, precipitated from a 20-foot rock by the horns of a furious ox, lay without motion at the bottom; he might well have been dead, or at least have a limb or two broken. He came to himself, and the cloud passed over without bad consequences. The carriage overturned by Aaron Delacourt in a ditch, but neither we nor it were disabled nor broken. Biscay and Guipuscon a perfect paradise, set off by the most brilliant weather. I was a good deal surprised to find all my Spanish unserviceable here, the people only understanding what they call Basque, which I have no doubt resembles Hindustani more than it does Spanish by a great deal. Valladolid, a nasty old town; Burgos, a very fine town, with an exquisite cathedral; Vittoria, a fine town, surrounded with such profuse and romantic beauty as beggars all description. We blessed God for all things on arriving at Bayonne, where we passed two or three days. My letters procured us leave to take Versailles in our way to Verdun and to stay there some days, and the General (Hedonville) explained to me that during the stay I might urge any claims or make use of any interest I could to effect my exchange, or, if I wished, in case of failure, to reside near Paris. He did not think that, in my position, it would be refused me to remain at Versailles, which I shall certainly endeavour to do, if I find it impossible to get away. Marshal Mortier, not content with his efforts to procure me my liberty, has recommended me to his friends in Paris, supplied me with cash at Madrid to prepare for my journey, and gave me besides a letter of credit for Paris to an unlimited amount. He told me he had not the smallest doubt of my procuring leave to return to England until my exchange could be effected. If I find that I cannot do this, I am confident he will make use of every means in his power, that the hopes he has given me may not be disappointed. We found everybody amiable and agreeable on our entry into France, where people seem to consider us with a sort of friendly distinction. We found no difficulties, were immediately left in the full enjoyment of our liberty, have put ourselves at our ease, consider ourselves travellers in France, and prepare to trace with a sort of triumph our considerable routes on the map of Europe. The contrast between being in unhappy Spain and in France, you will easily believe, is sufficiently remarkable—cheerful fires, palatable food, obliging manners, excellent inns, capital posting, claret and champagne, English scenery, burst upon us with all the graces of novelty, or rather of return after a long privation. As the carriage I had bought was not worse for wear, and was light and convenient for posting, we determined to travel as far as Bordeaux, and to continue it, if it did not prove too expensive. We find it as cheap as any other way, and so shall keep on to Versailles in the same agreeable way. We have nothing before us but good roads ; that between Bayonne and this is very heavy. The post is extremely well regulated, and travellers are protected from imposition or difficulty by purchasing the book of orders on that subject. We arrived here the day before yesterday at ten o'clock at night, and the next day again set forward. This city with its harbour is so superb and the town-plan so gigantic as completely to astonish us. If its wealth and prosperity were to go on and be promoted by peace and security of commerce, it would soon surpass in stately beauty London or any town that I have ever seen. Its grand theatre, erected with the highest architectural magnificence, shamed the dusky clay-built pile which, fortunately burnt, enclosed in such a metropolis as London one of the finest theatres in Europe—shamed the dusky clay-built pile of the Haymarket, that does enclose perhaps the most splendid assembly in the world. We dined yesterday with a wealthy merchant, to whom we were recommended by one of Bayonne, who took us by the hand, befriended us, and entertained us with his intelligent conversation merely to please himself. We went to the play in the evening ; the performance was mediocre, and the audience thin and not remarkable. We go to the play again to-night, and dine with the wealthy merchant again to-morrow. When I get to England again, you must make a point of writing to me very often, you and Gos ; I cannot bear the thoughts of being forgotten by you. Tell my chum Mudge not to forget me, for I am much attached to him. I wrote to him from Talavera, but by some accident I lost sight of the letter when I was making up my packet before leaving that place. Remember me very kindly to all brother-officers and friends. Make a point of going to General Sherbrooke and telling him that every anxiety for his welfare which his nearest and dearest friends can feel, I feel also. Tell him . . . I still have hopes of exchange. You will not forget to tell General Stewart that you have heard from me and General H. Campbell. I am still upon crutches; but if my stay in France is to be prolonged, I shall consult the Faculty at Paris respecting a wooden leg. May God bless and prosper you, my dear Mulcaster; and allow me always a high place in your affection, and do you always class me among the warmest, the most attached, the most grateful of your friends,

CHARLES BOOTHBY.

PARIS, 2nd March 1810.

MY DEAREST FATHER,—The first step is to procure permission to remain in Paris, which, although I have not yet received officially, I am given to understand will be granted. I shall then turn my attention with all my powers to procure either my exchange, or permission to go to England to endeavour to effect it there. I do not wish to raise hopes which perhaps might be disappointed, but I cannot persuade myself that I am doomed to a very long separation from you and all that I love. I am so well that I can enjoy all the sights of Paris. We are treated with the utmost liberality, even with distinction; and if I get amongst you soon I shall not regret the being captured, which has given me an opportunity of seeing things which perhaps may never offer again. Would to God I could hear something from you, three words would be sufficient; do try if you cannot just let me know that you are all well. Captain Stephens is very well, and I fancy will get leave to remain in Paris some time.—Ever, my dearest Father, your most devotedly affectionate son, CHARLES.

PARIS, 10th March 1810.

MY DEAREST FATHER, — I have made application, grounded upon my infirmity, to be allowed to come to England for a limited time, for the purpose of effecting my exchange, with the obligation to return in case of failure.

The success of this application is uncertain ; I therefore would recommend your casting about to discover whether it is impossible to forward it by any arrangement on your side the water. More exchanges between individuals have been effected by interest there than here.

The Abbé Dillon found me out the other day, and has made me acquainted with his sister, niece, etc., which is a great resource, as they are very agreeable and friendly people. I am perfectly well. In writing to me confine yourself simply to private and essential subjects, which would not be stopped or opened.—Yours,

CHARLES.

P.S.—My petition has not yet received any answer —which is so far in its favour, for those answers that come quick are generally negative. If you can find out any interest sufficient to draw out such a paper as I have mentioned, take care that I am not put down *2nd Captain*, which is a regimental distinction and does not interfere with army rank—mine being the same as that of all other captains according to date. Nothing is so dangerous as *a hitch* upon these occasions ; and if the French Minister thought that they wanted to underrate me in order to get me cheaper, he might stop all proceedings.

PARIS, 26th March 1810.

MY DEAREST FATHER,—When I tell you that I have no letter from home of a later date than the 14th September

1809, you will conceive that my anxiety to hear of you is painful. Write to me and address it to Messrs. Mallet Frères and Company, Bankers, Paris, and write "Mr. Boothby" at one corner of the direction ; then enclose it to Jos. Casenove and Company, Old Pay Office, Broad Street, London. You may seal your letter and talk to me at your ease on family affairs, but always so as that you would not mind if it were to be opened.

I gave a letter for you in charge two days ago to Major L'Estrange, who has got leave to effect his exchange. In that I told you that my hopes of coming to England shortly were increased, but that still I could not bid you to be sanguine ; the case remains as it was. An officer of rank, who was interested about my exchange, told me some days ago that it appeared my affair could be managed by means of the officer whom I, in my petition, had proposed to get sent for myself. I shall know more shortly.

I had the satisfaction of seeing the Emperor last Sunday at his chapel—a sight for which I had been very curious. I had an opportunity to observe him well for half an hour.

With my kindest love to all, I am ever, my dearest Father,   CHARLES.

PARIS, *Friday* 13*th April* 1810.

MY DEAREST LOU,[1]—I take every opportunity of writing to you, but the grievous silence in which you have all been enveloped since the 14th September 1809 is not yet broken. I hope, however, that you receive my letters, although some sour devil evidently makes yours to me

---

[1] Louisa Rafela Boothby, sister of Captain Boothby.

miscarry. I have seen all that was desirable in these vast fêtes which have celebrated the union between Napoleon and the Archduchess, and have seen them very close. I shall, I hope, be able to tell you all about these things before they are forgotten.

I cannot tell you how pleasant I find the society into which Arthur Dillon introduced me at the house of Madame de Boigne, his niece, who is a sweet, pretty little creature. Her mother, Madame D'Osmond, Monsieur D'Osmond, and Mr. Ernulf D'Osmond,—all these and many more are very choice people, and extend a familiar kindness to me, which makes my residence here much more agreeable. I am in a most enviable lodging, and see from my windows an old powdered gentleman, his lady, and their daughters, working in a very pretty tasty garden, that cheers me and puts me in mind of Edwinstowe. To be sure, there are some "tops"[1] in sight also, such as made Mamsey cry at Nottingham.

My health and spirits are just the same as they always have been. I go out less, but am for ever "cheerful and merry," never finding the day long enough for what I have to do and not do. The pain which I mentioned a long while ago as still remaining I cannot say is quite gone, but I am sensible that it is going, because at Madrid it used to plague me and break my sleep, whereas here I very seldom think of it, sleep all night, and never feel it in bed. I should not care twopence if it were always to remain as it is, but as I think it will go entirely, to be sure I make no objection. I talk of myself more than anything else, because I believe the subject interests you more than any other, thank thee.

[1] Chimney-pots, called "tops" by his mother before she could speak English perfectly.

Madame d'Osmond talks of dear Lady Milnes; give my best love to her and Sir Robert and every Nottinghamshire thing. Tell Jasper that I have been apprised that the Minister of War has received my petition favourably, and has laid it before the Emperor, for whose decision the affair waits. H.M. may say "no," but in truth I cannot think he will.

All doubt is at an end. My petition is assented to by the Emperor; but from some vacation in the offices I am told that it will be yet a month before I shall receive my passport, perhaps more, so that I should place my arrival somewhere about the middle of June at latest. My mind is now easy, if I could but get letters from you. God bless thee, my lass,   CHARLES.

PARIS, 24th April 1810.

MY EVER DEAREST FATHER,—I cannot express to you the load that your letters of the 1st February and 9th April have taken off my mind; the latter I received last night, so that nothing can do better than the mode of communication I have pointed out, and as it came sealed, you may write with more freedom about ourselves, not considering it as at all likely to be opened, but avoiding all subjects of a political nature to guard against a possibility. I hope to get amongst you time enough to see the garden dressed in the beauties of summer. Nobody loves that garden so much as Rafela[1] and myself. I wrote to Billy[2] the other day to desire that he would find out the Commissioners for the Transport Board, to ascertain and if possible obviate any objections to the liberation of Captain Meseure, against whom the

---

[1] His mother.   [2] His brother.

Emperor, at my own request, has authorised my exchange. I was advised to make my petition as definite as possible, and therefore proposed the French officer above mentioned as of the same rank and the corresponding branch of service. The proposal, I know, has been made by the French Government, and I have no doubt I should be immediately liberated if the British Government would certify its acceptance of it. I wish Billy to find out if there be any hesitation about it, and if there be, to give in immediately a written statement representing that the nomination of Captain Meseure was made by me in my petition to the Minister of War, and did not proceed from any suggestion from the French War Office, but merely from my inquiring if there was any Captain of Engineers in England against whom I could propose myself in exchange; but if there will not be any hesitation let nothing be said about it. In the meantime I have written to ask permission to depart immediately, and am not at all certain that it will be refused.—Your ever dutiful and affectionate   CHARLES.

P.S.—*26th April.* I have not got any answer to my request to be allowed to come to England on parole.

Letter from Major William Boothby to his son
Captain Charles Boothby

EDWINSTOWE, 20*th May.*
(Received in PARIS, 29*th May.*)

MY DEAREST CHARLES,—I send you a copy of a letter I have just received from Lord Newark in answer to one I wrote to him on receiving yours of the 20th April.

"On the receipt of your last letter I lost not a moment in sending it to Mr. Douglas, fearing, however,

at the same time, that although definitive as to its object,
it might be thought indefinite as to the means by which
that object was to be obtained. The event has proved me
in the right, as Mr. Douglas, whom I saw yesterday
morning, informs me that it is impossible for the Transport Board to release the officer mentioned in Charles's
letter, unless they receive some official intimation from
the French Government that your son's liberation shall.
immediately follow, and no such intimation, either private
or public, has yet been received. The steps that have been
already taken by the Transport Board are as follows. They
sent several weeks since two certificates to Paris. By the
one they engaged to release an officer of equal rank
upon Charles being permitted to come home to England;
by the other, that they would immediately release any
officer of equal rank, upon an assurance that Boothby
should be released upon the appearance of that officer in
France. But to neither of these propositions have they
received an answer."

Mr. Douglas belongs to the Transport Board. I hope
amid these circumstances there can be no doubt that you
will soon be able to avail yourself of the kindness you
have received on both sides of the water. Your letter gave
us much delight by telling us you had at last received
intelligence from us. All your friends are well, and desire
their kindest love to you, my dearest Charles.—Your ever
truly affectionate,   ' W. BOOTHBY.

Letter from Duchesse de Fitz-James to Madame d'Osmond

PARIS, *le* 15 *Juin.*

Je vous envois, ma chère, la lettre que je reçois du
Ministre de la Guerre. Je pense que déjà vous savez

peut-être ce qu'elle m'annonce, mais dans l'incertitude je vous l'adresse toujours, heureuse si je pouvais croire avoir un peu contribué à la réussite d'une chose que vous désirez.

PARIS, le 18 Juin 1810.

Le Ministre de la Guerre présente ses hommages respectueux à Madame de Fitz-James, et a l'honneur de lui annoncer que M. le Capitaine Anglais Boothby auquel elle veut bien s'intéresser recevra un passeport pour retourner sur sa parole dans sa patrie, dès qu'il se présentera dans les Bureaux du Ministre.

Letter from Madame d'Osmond to Captain Charles Boothby

BEAUREGARD, le 16 Juin 1810.

C'est avec une grande joie, mon cher Monsieur Boothby, que je vous adresse les incluses—retournez, retournez dans votre heureuse patrie, que je regrette tous les jours de ma vie ; vous y trouverez le bonheur que vous méritez, mes vœux et mon tendre intérêt vous y accompagneront.—Je suis bien fâchée que vous n'avez pas donné quelques jours à Beauregard avant votre départ. Si vous rencontrez mon frère Edouard, parlez lui de nous tous et de notre tendre amitié pour lui et pour toute sa famille. J'espère que la robe que vous portez à Georgina ne vous causera pas d'embarras. Monsieur d'Osmond et F.-J. partagent tous mes sentiments pour vous. Mademoiselle de Boigne est à Paris.

Letter from Captain Charles Boothby to his Father and Mother

July 1810.

This letter will be a little satisfaction for my beloved Father and Mother.

Madame d'Osmond, engaging in my behalf the ci-devant Duchess de Fitz-James, succeeded at last in getting me permission to come home on parole, engaging myself to return at the expiration of three months, if I failed in procuring the release of Monsieur Meseure, in which I suppose there will be no difficulty from Lord Newark's letter which you sent me. I confess, my dear old Dad, I have some little uneasiness at the thoughts of our meeting, arising from a feeling which perhaps does you injustice. If, like me, you have trained your ideas rather to be rejoiced at blessings which still remain to me, and promise to make my life happy, than to repine at the blow my youth has sustained, then, indeed, our joy at meeting will be unalloyed ; and I will hope for this triumph of your philosophy over your tenderness. I have told you that I am still on crutches, which gives me an appearance of helplessness that does not at all belong to my health and strength. The remedy I shall find in London will, I anxiously hope, do away almost entirely with this appearance. If I thought less of your piety and temper to make the best of things, I would recommend you to defer our meeting until after I can walk, but as it is, if I find my apprenticeship will be very long, I will certainly take a trip to Notts to satisfy our mutual impatience. But write to tell me all your feelings on this head, Mamsey's and Lou's. I am not afraid of the brothers and sisters so much as the fathers and mothers ; but, my crutches apart, I believe you will not find the slightest alteration. But in your joy at my return keep in mind that you are to see me on crutches. If you don't see me in high spirits, which are natural to me, you may be sure that it is because I see you not reconciled to my misfortune. After all, my darlings of Edwinstowe, there is no use in saying anything more about it. I doubt not we shall pull through, and shall be guided by the letter which I shall find from you at the Blenheim.—Yours ever,   CHARLES.

*Letter from Captain Charles Boothby to the
Marêchal Duc de Trevise* [1]

MORLAIX, 2nd *July* 1810.

MY LORD,—In the very hour which precedes my embarkation, I sit down to take my leave of Your Excellency in a manner which, though hurried, carries with it a strong appearance of sincerity, and I beseech you to forgive whatever may be wanting in form, and believe at least that my intention is to express every sense of gratitude and regard which your uncommon goodness to me ought naturally to call forth. I address Your Excellency no longer as a prisoner who may derive benefit from your protection, or freedom from your influence. Before this reaches you I shall be in my own country beyond the reach of your extensive benevolence; and although I do not doubt but the candour of your character always gave credit to my expressions of gratitude, yet I cannot but be pleased with the moment in which I can offer thanks that cannot be suspected of design, or as the inviter of further favours.

My Lord, I can never forget the voice of kindness that, in moments of desolation, penetrated the abode of sickness and infirmity. It had a cheering sound, whose impression is at this moment fresh upon my heart and revives that series of unlimited favours, which my unfortunate situation afterwards moved you to heap upon me, not one particular of which is it possible for me to

[1] Le Maréchal de l'Empire Mortier.

forget. They have terminated in restoring me to my own country, whither I am now going on parole for the purpose of effecting my exchange.

It is scarcely permitted to me to hope that I can ever make any other return, as in my own country I am devoid of that rank and influence which has enabled Your Excellency to be so essentially my protector; but should the good fortune of any such occasion present itself, in executing your wishes I shall ever consider myself as performing the most agreeable of duties. I should not omit to mention that Colonel Montfort's attachment to Your Excellency has led him to assist me with the most good-natured zeal.

I have the honour to be, my Lord, with the most distinguished respect and attachment, Your Grace's most obedient, humble servant,   CHARLES BOOTHBY,
                                        Capitaine du Génie.

Letter from Captain Charles Boothby to the Maréchal Duc de Trevise

NEWCASTLE-ON-TYNE, 11th *May* 1814.

MY LORD DUKE,—A British officer, who, having lost a leg at the battle of Talavera, had the good fortune to fall into your gracious hands, begs permission to recall himself to Your Excellency as a person bound to you by gratitude and affection.

During the reign of the Emperor Napoleon, I would not allow myself the liberty of addressing you, lest any communication from England might by possibility subject to suspicion a character, which its great elevation made so obvious to remark. But now that all the world seems to reclaim the voice of confidence and joy,

I cannot longer deny to my heart the relief of breaking its long silence, to beg that Your Excellency will not, after having fastened so indelibly upon my memory the impression of your benevolence, yourself forget that I have a right to hear and to repeat your name with interest and pleasure.

That I have never heard or repeated it with opposite sensations (though often indeed with anxiety), I count amongst the things for which I ought most to be thankful.

It would have seemed too much to hope that I should never *in this country* hear one of the most conspicuous officers of Napoleon mentioned with dislike. Yet more than this has been accorded to my feelings, for throughout this free-speaking country the name of Mortier is repeated with affection ; and never, amidst all the tremendous scenes in which it has been so eminent, since it became interesting to me, have I had to vindicate it from the censures of my countrymen, or to lament that the part which circumstances had imposed on my illustrious protector was unsuited to the nobleness of his nature. On the contrary, after seeing him conduct his share of the war, always in its most generous character, it has been to me a triumph that he was the last to quit the side of his fallen master, and the first to be honoured with the confidence of him newly risen.

Would it seem, my Lord, by the freedom of my language that I am forgetting the rank of the person I address, let your goodness attribute it rather to my remembering so well the reasons I have to rejoice in all that may redound to his fame and honour.

Indeed, I cannot much fear to offend him, while conscious that my pen is guided by nothing worse than

the most unfeigned respect for his character, and the
purest gratitude for an unmeasured kindness towards my
misfortunes, the recollection of which can even persuade
me that he will not deem impertinent some mention of
that humble individual, for whose welfare he so effectually
exerted his powerful means.

Before I quitted France I addressed to Your Excellency a letter from Morlaix, which I hope you received,
as it would not only assure you of my gratitude, but also
give your kind heart the satisfaction of knowing that
your protection had been complete and effectual in my
behalf. It secured me from every difficulty arising from
a want of communication with England, to which (my
country) it soon effected my return to dry the tears of
my father and mother, and to restore their happiness by
showing them that mine was not destroyed. By habit,
and by the ingenuity of our mechanics, I have recovered
much bodily activity. On horseback I am perfectly at
ease. I walk with facility without a stick, and am
grateful to find how little I have lost of life's enjoyments.

That *all her enjoyments*, my good Lord Duke, may very
long be continued to you ; and that, when at last those
cease, better and more perfect may await you, is the
sincere and earnest wish of Your Excellency's most
faithful and gratefully attached servant,

CHARLES BOOTHBY,
Captain Royal Engineers.

Letter from the Maréchal Duc de Trevise to
Captain Charles Boothby

AU CHÂTEAU DU PLESSIS LALANDE,
le 22 Juin 1814.

MONSIEUR,—J'ai reçu avec un véritable plaisir votre

lettre du 11 mai ; celle que vous m'avez écrite de Morlaix, en quittant la France, ne m'est jamais parvenue.
Il ne m'a point été indifférent d'apprendre que malgré
vos longues souffrances, et la nature d'une blessure aussi
grave, vous étiez parvenu au point de faire avec facilité
tous les exercices du corps ; vous ne pouviez rien
m'apprendre qui me fut plus agréable, car jamais je ne
vous ai perdu de vue ; et l'intérêt bien senti que vous
m'avez inspiré m'a constamment porté à demander de vos
nouvelles toutes les fois que j'en ai trouvé l'occasion.
J'appris donc avec une vive satisfaction d'un officier Anglais,
avec lequel je dînais il y a environs deux mois chez
Lord Castlereagh, que vous jouïssiez d'une bonne santé ;
puisse le ciel vous accorder une série de jours heureux au
sein de votre respectable famille. Je me figure tout le
bonheur que doivent maintenant éprouver Madame votre
mère et M. votre père ; je me le figure par celui que
j'éprouve moi-même près de ma femme et de mes
enfans, après une aussi longue et une aussi pénible
séparation.

J'espère que vous n'avez pas renoncé au désir de revoir
le continent : il me serait alors bien agréable de vous voir
chez moi ; j'aurais beaucoup de plaisir à vous présenter à
ma famille.

Veuillez, mon cher Monsieur Charles, agréer l'assurance de ma considération distinguée et de mon attache-
ment.

9 781104 367916